# delish
## kids
### (SUPER-AWESOME, CRAZY-FUN, BEST-EVER)
# COOKBOOK

Joanna Saltz & the Editors of Delish

KIDS
HEARST
HOME

# Contents

# What's Inside

---

What a normal weekend looks like: me and my kids, Everett, Teddy, and Spencer (from left), fighting over who gets the first cookie bar.

Me at 5 years old with my priorities in check

My mom in the kitchen circa 1976

# Trust me: Cooking is easy.

My mom taught me that. To be clear, she was not someone who spent her weekends baking or teaching me the culinary basics. She worked full-time running her own company, which was a lot to juggle——but every night, she would come home late after a long day, walk straight into the kitchen, and whip up some kind of dinner using whatever she could find in the house. **"I need a show called *Cooking in My Coat*," she would joke.**

Not everything came out great—— oftentimes her recipes were a work in progress. But even as a little girl, I was always amazed by watching her ingenuity, like using a jar of marinara sauce as a shortcut base for tomato soup. Little did I know, it would start me on a path to creating Delish. I may never have learned how to properly cut an onion, but she instilled in me this relaxed feeling that cooking doesn't have to be perfect…or stressful…or precious. The point was to get in there and try——and it's what I tell my own kids now.

That's what I hope this book teaches you: confidence. It doesn't matter if you chop like a pro or know what "sous vide" means (a list of words worth knowing starts on page 6). But it also doesn't mean that as a kid, you're limited to silly recipes (you'll be shocked to discover how easy it is to whip up homemade brownies, page 132). Use our directions, take a leap, and make a thing. You can do this, and we can help you.

Let's get started.

Love,

5

# Important Terms to Know

## A

**Al dente**
An Italian term meaning perfectly cooked pasta: tender but slightly firm. (Not mushy!)

## B

**Beat**
To vigorously stir a mixture, such as whisking eggs with a fork to make scrambled eggs or using a stand mixer or hand mixer to combine the butter and sugar for cookie dough.

**Bloom**
To heat dry spices with a fat (butter or oil) to make them more flavorful and aromatic.

**Boil**
To heat a liquid until it bubbles rapidly. You cook pasta in boiling water (which is 212°F).

**Broil**
To cook food under direct, intense heat. Every oven has a broiler! It's located at either the top or bottom of the appliance.

## C

**Chop**
To cut food into smaller, similarly sized pieces (about the size of peas) so that everything cooks at the same rate.

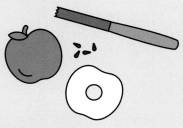

**Core**
To remove seeds and tough centers from fruits (apples, pears) and vegetables (bell peppers).

**Cream**
To beat together butter and sugar until well combined and lighter in color. It's an important step for a fluffy cake.

**Cross-contamination**
When bacteria from one food is transferred to another object—often from raw meat. This can cause you to get sick, which is why it's extra important to wash your hands and keep kitchen tools clean. (See page 9.)

## D

**Deglaze**
To unstick food on a hot pan by pouring liquid into it and scraping the bottom with a wooden spoon. (Well-cooked, stuck-to-the-bottom bits of food = loaded with delicious flavor.)

**Divided**
When an ingredient amount is followed by "divided," it means that you're using some of the ingredient at different stages of the recipe.

**Double boiler**
Equipment used to gently cook, or heat food without the risk of burning. To set up a double boiler, nestle a heatproof bowl over a pot of simmering water.

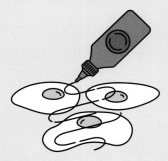

**Drizzle**
To pour a thin stream of a liquid ingredient (like olive oil, hot sauce, or melted chocolate) back and forth over a dish. It's usually a finishing touch that looks fancy.

## E

**Emulsify**
To mix together two liquids that usually don't combine easily—like oil and vinegar to make dressing.

## F

**Fold**
To very gently mix ingredients into a batter or dough, usually with a silicone spatula.

## G

**Grease**
To coat a baking sheet or pan with a fat such as butter or nonstick cooking spray to avoid food sticking to the cookware.

## H

**Hangry**
A state of anger caused by hunger. Which is why breakfast is so important! Skipping it can make you extra hangry.

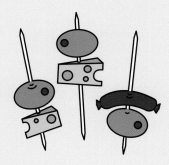

**Hors d'oeuvres**
The French term to describe appetizers, or small savory bites, typically finger foods.

## I

**Icebox cake**
A no-bake dessert composed of layers of cookies and whipped cream that spends a lot of time in the refrigerator. While it chills, the crunchy cookies soften to become cake-like in texture. (See page 134.)

## J

**Julienne**
A fancy way to describe cutting foods into thin strips about 2 inches long. Like the carrot and cucumbers in the Shrimp Summer Rolls (page 64).

## K

**Knead**
To work dough ingredients until you form a smooth and pliable mass. Kneading by hand means pressing and folding the dough with the heel of your hand over and over, like in our pizza dough recipe on page 94. It's easy but it takes some time (and muscle). To make the job easier, you can use the dough hook attachment of a stand mixer.

**Kosher salt**
We call for this ingredient a lot in this book. Kosher salt has slightly larger crystals than iodized salt (the type that you generally find in a salt shaker). It's also iodine-free. (Iodized salt can have an unpleasant taste.)

## L

**"Let rest."**
It's an instruction we'll tell you after you've cooked meat. Letting your chicken or steak sit for 10 to 15 minutes before slicing will ensure that all the juices don't escape onto your cutting board while cutting the meat.

## M

**Mince**
To cut a food into super-tiny pieces—about the size of sesame seeds.

## N

**Nonstick pan**
A skillet with a slippery coating to ensure foods don't stick to it. Aka your secret weapon when flipping pancakes (page 176).

## O

**Opaque**
When your food is no longer see-through. When shrimp turns from translucent (allowing light to pass through) to an opaque pink—which it will do super fast!—it's cooked through.

**Oven-safe**
Kitchen equipment that can be safely used in an oven, such as a cast-iron skillet. (One of our favorite things to cook with.)

## P

**Pinch**
A small measurement of an ingredient (often salt or spices) that you can hold between your thumb and pointer finger.

**Piping**
To use a pastry bag or resealable plastic bag (with the corner snipped off) to distribute frosting (such as buttercream) in a controlled and/or decorative way.

## Q

**Quarter**
To cut an ingredient into four equal-size pieces.

## R

**Reduce**
The process of thickening a liquid such as a sauce or stock by boiling or simmering until the liquid has reduced in volume and intensified in flavor.

**Roast**
A method of cooking using the dry heat of an oven.

## S

**Sauté**
To cook food in a small amount of fat over relatively high heat.

**"Season to taste."**
To alter the flavor of a dish by tasting and adding more ingredients (most often salt) according to personal preferences.

**Simmer**
To heat a liquid to just below a boil.

**Stiff peaks/soft peaks**
To whip an ingredient (such as egg whites or heavy cream) until it has increased in volume and become stiff, leaving behind a "peak" after removing beaters or a whisk. The tips of stiff peaks stand up straight, while the tips of soft peaks curl over.

## T

**Tender**
When cooked until tender, a food has become soft enough that it is easily cut with a knife or chewed.

**Toss**
To combine ingredients gently to avoid damaging or altering their shape, size, or texture.

## U

**Underbake**
To remove a baked good from the oven before it has finished cooking. In cakes and quick breads, underbaking will result in sunken centers and uncooked batter. Gooey, underbaked cookies aren't the worst thing in the world though.

## V

**Vegetarian**
A person who does not eat meat and possibly other animal by-products (like broth), often for moral (such as environmental), ethical, religious, health, or dietary reasons.

## W

**Whip**
The process of beating food using a whisk, hand mixer, or stand mixer, to incorporate air and increase volume. The most satisfying and delicious example: whipped cream.

**Whisk**
The process of incorporating ingredients using a wire whisk or fork.

## X

**XOXO**
The way you might sign a thank-you letter to whomever bought you this book.

## Y

**Yeast**
The scientific definition: a very tiny fungus that turns sugar into alcohol and carbon dioxide, a gas that causes rising. In baking, active dry yeast, instant yeast, and fresh yeast are most common. Each of these will cause baked goods to rise as well as add a distinct flavor and texture.

## Z

**Zest**
To remove the outer rind of a citrus fruit for use. When removing the zest (most often with a small grater), be sure to remove only the colored outer rind—the white layer beneath it is bitter!

# You Can Handle It!

We've rated each recipe on a scale of difficulty. Don't be afraid to try anything. You've got this!

**BEGINNER   PRO-IN-TRAINING   PRO**

Anyone can make the recipe. You don't need much (or any) experience.

**BEGINNER   PRO-IN-TRAINING   PRO**

These recipes take a little more effort, and some grown-up assistance is likely required.

**BEGINNER   PRO-IN-TRAINING   PRO**

You'll definitely want an adult to help you. These recipes involve more technique, whether it be in knife skills, stovetop cooking, decorating, or all of the above.

# Yes, There Are a Few Rules

We don't like to keep things too uptight when we're cooking, but there are some guidelines to follow before you get started.

## Clean hands are a chef's best tool.

Your hands are the ultimate multitasker in the kitchen. Wash your hands often while you're cooking—before you get started, after dealing with raw meat (to avoid cross-contamination), before serving other people, and before eating.

## Keep things tidy!

Wiping down the counter, washing kitchen tools as you use them, and putting away ingredients when you're done measuring them will help minimize the mess.

## Always ask an adult for help...

...when dealing with hot or sharp things. Even if it's something you've done before, it's always a good idea to have a grown-up in the kitchen with you.

## Spoon and level.

Scooping straight from the flour container can result in denser baked goods. Spoon the flour into the measuring cup, then level it off with the flat side of a butter knife.

## Read the recipe all the way through first—at least twice!

There's nothing more stressful than realizing midway through the recipe that you weren't prepared for a challenging (or a very time-consuming) step such as letting a cheesecake chill for at least 5 hours before slicing into it! Things will go more smoothly if you know the whole process.

## Prep!

Organizing your ingredients beforehand will make the whole process easier. In this book, you'll find the ingredients listed first so that before you start chopping or measuring, you can gather everything you need.

## When in doubt, use a thermometer.

When cooking meat, it's the easiest and safest way to make sure everything is cooked through and safe to eat. In time, you'll memorize these internal temperatures:
- **Beef:** 145°F
- **Chicken:** 165°F
- **Pork:** 145°F

## Wash your fruits and veggies.

To remove dirt, harmful bacteria, and/or pesticides, it's important to rinse off fresh produce. The opposite is true for meat. Washing it can actually lead to cross-contamination!

## Season, season, season.

We rarely call for specific salt and pepper measurements when it comes to savory dishes because everyone has different taste preferences and dietary restrictions. When your dish is almost finished (and after the meat, if there is any, is cooked), taste it. If it's bland, you probably want to add more salt. Start with a pinch (or ¼ teaspoon), stir it in, and give it a try. Then repeat if necessary. Remember, you can always add more, but you can't take any out.

## Have fun!

Don't be afraid to mess up. Your food doesn't need to look picture-perfect for it to be absolutely delicious. And sometimes it takes a few times to get a dish to just the way you like it best.

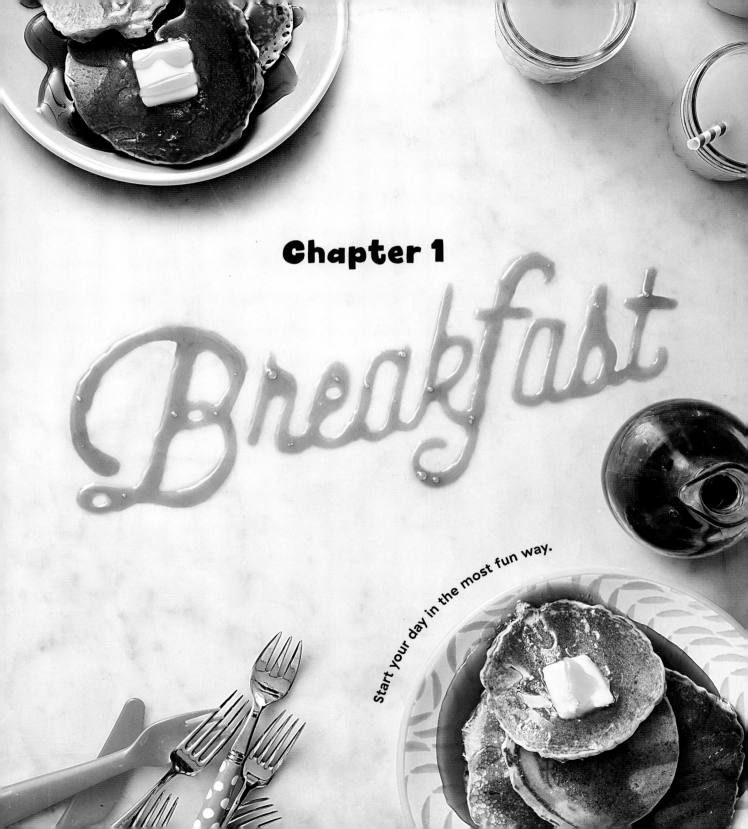

# Chapter 1

## Breakfast

Start your day in the most fun way.

# Banana Split Oatmeal

**Serves 1 • Total Time: 10 minutes**

BEGINNER          PRO-IN-TRAINING          PRO

Give oatmeal an ice–cream–sundae–inspired makeover. Nothing will brighten your morning like rainbow sprinkles.

| Ingredients | Amount |
| --- | --- |
| Milk (any kind) or water | ½ cup |
| Old–fashioned rolled oats | 1 cup |
| Kosher salt | Pinch |
| Banana | ½, sliced |
| Chopped walnuts | 2 tablespoons |
| Mini chocolate chips | 1 tablespoon |
| Rainbow sprinkles | For topping |
| Maraschino cherry | 1, for topping |

**1.** In a medium saucepan over high heat, bring milk (or water) to a boil. Stir in oats and salt with a wooden spoon, reduce heat to low, and simmer until oats are tender and creamy, 5 minutes.

**2.** Serve oatmeal in a bowl topped with banana, walnuts, chocolate chips, sprinkles, and a cherry on top, of course!

## What You'll Need

Medium Saucepan

Wooden Spoon

# Apple Pancake Dippers

**Makes 16 • Total Time: 10 minutes**

BEGINNER      PRO-IN-TRAINING      PRO

Eating with your hands is always more fun than using a fork and knife. (Even adults would agree.)

| Ingredients | Amount |
| --- | --- |
| Pancake mix | Follow directions for preparing about **14 pancakes** |
| Apples | **4, sliced into rounds** |
| Cooking spray | **For pan** |
| Cinnamon sugar | **½ cup** |
| Maple syrup | **For dipping** |

We like using Honeycrisp, Pink Lady, or Jonagold apples because they're sweet and crisp.

**What You'll Need**

Large Bowl

Whisk

Melon Baller

Cutting Board

Tongs

Large Nonstick Skillet

Turner

Small Bowl

1. Make pancake batter according to package instructions.

2. Using a melon baller, scoop out core from apple slices.

3. Toss apple slices in pancake batter until they are completely coated.

4. Meanwhile, heat a large nonstick skillet over medium heat and grease with cooking spray. Working in batches, add a few dredged apple slices and cook undisturbed until bubbles form on pancake batter, 2 minutes. Flip and cook 2 minutes more. Repeat with remaining apple slices.

5. Transfer apple pancakes to a bowl of cinnamon sugar and toss while warm. Serve with maple syrup.

# Chocolate Chip Muffins

**Makes 16 · Total Time: 40 minutes**

BEGINNER — PRO-IN-TRAINING — PRO

They're best fresh out of the oven, while the chips are nice and melty. Just like a chocolate chip cookie!

| Ingredients | Amount |
| --- | --- |
| All-purpose flour | 2 cups |
| Kosher salt | 1 teaspoon |
| Baking powder | 1 teaspoon |
| Baking soda | ½ teaspoon |
| Butter | ½ cup (1 stick), softened |
| Granulated sugar | ½ cup |
| Brown sugar | ¼ cup, packed |
| Large egg | 1 |
| Pure vanilla extract | 1 teaspoon |
| Whole milk | 1 cup |
| Semisweet chocolate chips | 1 cup |

**What You'll Need**

2 Muffin Tins

Muffin Liners

2 Large Bowls

Whisk

Mixer

Spatula

Toothpick

Oven Mitts

**1.** Preheat oven to 350°F and line two muffin tins with liners. In a large bowl, whisk together flour, salt, baking powder, and baking soda.

**2.** In another large bowl using a hand mixer or in the bowl of a stand mixer, beat butter and sugars together until light and fluffy. Add egg and vanilla and beat until combined.

**3.** Add half of dry ingredients to wet ingredients and mix until just combined, then add milk and mix. Add in remaining dry ingredients and mix until just combined, then fold in chocolate chips with a spatula.

**4.** Divide batter evenly among muffin liners and bake until a toothpick inserted in the middle comes out clean, 23 to 25 minutes.

**FYI!**
Adding the dry ingredients gradually helps make these muffins extra fluffy.

# Cinnamon Rolls

**Makes 1 dozen • Total Time: 3 hours 25 minutes**

BEGINNER          PRO-IN-TRAINING          PRO

These classic cinnamon rolls might take a while, but they're SO worth it. The result is gooey, fluffy, and totally amazing.

| Ingredients | Amount |
| --- | --- |
| **For the dough** | |
| Cooking spray | For bowl and pan |
| Whole milk | 1 cup, warm |
| Instant yeast | 1 (0.25-ounce) packet |
| Large eggs | 2, at room temperature |
| Butter | 5 tablespoons, softened |
| All-purpose flour | 4½ cups, plus more for surface |
| Kosher salt | 2 teaspoons |
| Granulated sugar | ½ cup |
| Baking soda | ¼ teaspoon |
| **For the filling** | |
| Butter | ½ cup (1 stick), softened |
| Brown sugar | ¾ cup, packed |
| Ground cinnamon | 2 tablespoons |
| Kosher salt | ½ teaspoon |
| Ground nutmeg | ¼ teaspoon |
| **For the frosting** | |
| Cream cheese | 6 ounces, softened |
| Butter | ½ cup (1 stick), softened |
| Powdered sugar | 1 cup |
| Kosher salt | Pinch |
| Pure vanilla extract | 1 teaspoon |
| Whole milk or heavy cream | ¼ cup |

1. **Make dough:** Lightly grease a large bowl and a 9x13–inch pan with cooking spray. In the bowl of a stand mixer using the dough attachment, mix milk and yeast until yeast is mostly dissolved. On low speed, add in all remaining dough ingredients until combined.

2. Turn up speed to medium high and mix until a smooth, soft dough forms and starts to pull away from the sides of the bowl, 15 to 18 minutes. Transfer to greased bowl and turn dough several times so that all sides of dough are greased. Cover bowl with a clean kitchen towel and let rise until almost doubled, 1½ to 2 hours.

3. **Meanwhile, make filling:** In the bowl of a stand mixer using the paddle attachment, beat together filling ingredients until light and fluffy, 3 to 4 minutes.

4. Preheat oven to 400°F. Turn dough out onto a lightly floured surface and dust with more flour. Roll out into an 18–inch square, and spread with filling to the edges. Roll the dough into a log and cut into 12 pieces, each about 1½ inches thick.

5. Place rolls cut side up in baking pan. Cover with kitchen towel and let rise again until almost doubled, 30 to 40 minutes.

6. Bake until golden, 20 to 22 minutes.

7. **Meanwhile, make frosting:** In the bowl of a stand mixer using the paddle attachment, beat together cream cheese and butter until light and fluffy. Add powdered sugar, salt, and vanilla and beat until smooth. Gradually add milk (or heavy cream) to thin frosting.

8. Remove cinnamon rolls from oven and immediately spread frosting over rolls. Serve warm.

> If you don't have a stand mixer, you can knead the dough by hand. You'll know it's done when it's no longer sticky and it slowly bounces back when you poke a finger into it, about 20 minutes.

# The Super-Fun History of
# CINNAMON ROLLS

Nearly every European country has its own version of a sweet, doughy, breakfast roll. There's England's Chelsea bun and the German "Schnecken", but Swedish bakers are commonly credited with first adding cinnamon to buns in the 1700s. They called the baked good "Kanelbullar", and it was similar to the modern-day cinnamon roll.

Cinnamon first traveled to Europe from its native Sri Lanka in the 13th century, when **Italian explorer Marco Polo opened up the spice trade.**

German and Swedish immigrants in America continued to make their homelands' pastries, passing along recipes without an official name. **It wasn't until 1922 that the term "cinnamon roll" was coined in the U.S. by cookbook editors at** *Good Housekeeping.*

**The classic icing drizzled on top of the spice-filled buns is made from butter, sugar, vanilla, cream cheese, and a bit of citrus zest.** Many bakers like to put their own spin on the traditional icing, adding fruity jam spreads, chocolate sauce, or super-sweet caramel.

There's one thing everyone agrees on, though, and that's how to shape a cinnamon roll. It's simple: **You roll out your dough as flat as possible, slather it with cinnamony filling, roll it up nice and tight, slice into individual swirls, and watch them rise as they bake!**

**Cinnabon—a restaurant chain dedicated solely to cinnamon rolls—is famous for its buns' sweet-and-spicy scent.** The aroma has been used to make candles, air fresheners, and even lip balm.

People celebrate their love of cinnamon rolls in wacky ways. In 2018, **Wolferman's Bakery broke the Guinness World Record in Oregon for the largest cinnamon roll, at 1,149.7 pounds.** That's the weight of a full-grown moose!

# Cardamom

Before it's ground, cardamom has green or black pods. Green pods are often used in sweet dishes. Black pods are better for savory dishes. You can grind the spice yourself or you can buy it ground in the spice aisle.

**What You'll Need**

Blender

# Mango Lassi Smoothie Bowls

**Serves 2 • Total Time: 10 minutes**

BEGINNER          PRO-IN-TRAINING          PRO

These colorful smoothie bowls are inspired by the popular Indian yogurt–based drink. The flavors here are pretty traditional (the cardamom is key), but the berries on top are just for fun.

| Ingredients | Amount |
| --- | --- |
| **Frozen mango chunks** | **2 cups** |
| **Plain yogurt** | **⅓ cup** |
| **Ground cardamom** | **¼ teaspoon** |
| **Coconut milk** | **⅓ cup** |
| **Roasted unsalted pistachios** | **1 tablespoon, chopped** |
| **Mixed berries** | **¼ cup** |

**1.** Add mango to a blender and blend for 1 minute, until mango has broken down into smaller pieces.

**2.** Add yogurt, cardamom, and coconut milk and blend until smooth and creamy.

**3.** Divide mixture between bowls and top with pistachios and berries.

# Fruity Pebble French Toast

Serves 4 • Total Time: 20 minutes

BEGINNER     PRO-IN-TRAINING     PRO

Not only does this colorful cereal add an epic crunch to each bite, but it adds plenty of extra sweetness too. We know it's hard, but consider going easy on the maple syrup.

| Ingredients | Amount |
| --- | --- |
| Large eggs | 3 |
| Whole milk | 1 cup |
| Pure vanilla extract | 1 teaspoon |
| Ground cinnamon | ½ teaspoon |
| Fruity Pebbles | 3 cups |
| Sandwich bread | 8 slices |
| Butter | 4 tablespoons |
| Whipped cream | For serving |

1. In a shallow bowl, whisk together eggs, milk, vanilla, and cinnamon until combined. Add Fruity Pebbles to a separate shallow bowl.

2. Working one slice at a time, dip bread into egg mixture until fully soaked, about 45 seconds. Transfer soaked bread to Fruity Pebbles and press to coat, using your hands.

3. In a large skillet over medium-low heat, melt 2 tablespoons butter. Add 2 slices French toast and cook 3 minutes per side. Repeat with remaining butter and French toast slices.

4. Serve with whipped cream.

**What You'll Need**

2 Shallow Bowls

Whisk

Large Skillet

Turner

This recipe also works with crushed Cinnamon Toast Crunch, Frosted Flakes, Golden Grahams, or Cap'n Crunch!

# Party Pancakes

**Serves 6 · Total Time: 40 minutes**

BEGINNER     PRO-IN-TRAINING     PRO

Making pancakes for a crowd has never been so easy! Customize each quadrant with your family's favorite pancake toppings.

| Ingredients | Amount |
| --- | --- |
| **For the pancake base** | |
| Cooking spray | For pan |
| All-purpose flour | 2¼ cups |
| Granulated sugar | ¼ cup |
| Baking powder | 2 teaspoons |
| Baking soda | ½ teaspoon |
| Kosher salt | 1 teaspoon |
| Large eggs | 2 |
| Buttermilk | 2 cups |
| Butter | 4 tablespoons, melted |
| Maple syrup | For serving |
| **For Cinnamon Bun Pancake** | |
| Brown sugar | ⅓ cup, packed |
| Butter | 2 tablespoons, melted |
| Ground cinnamon | 2 teaspoons |
| **For Peanut Butter-Banana Pancake** | |
| Banana | 1, cut into coins |
| Peanut butter | 2 tablespoons |
| **For Strawberry-Chocolate Chip Pancake** | |
| Sliced strawberries | ¾ cup |
| Semisweet chocolate chips | ¼ cup |
| **For Blueberry-Lemon Pancake** | |
| Blueberries | ½ cup |
| Lemon zest | ¼ teaspoon |

### What You'll Need

Large Rimmed Baking Sheet

Medium Bowl

Whisk

Large Bowl

Spatula

2 Small Bowls

Resealable Plastic Bag

Chef's Knife

Oven Mitts

Peanut Butter-Banana Pancake

Blueberry-Lemon Pancake

**Strawberry-Chocolate Chip Pancake**

**Cinnamon Bun Pancake**

**1.** Preheat oven to 450°F. Grease a large rimmed baking sheet with cooking spray.

**2.** In a medium bowl, whisk together flour, sugar, baking powder, baking soda, and salt. In a large bowl, whisk together eggs, buttermilk, and melted butter. Add dry ingredients to wet ingredients and fold, just until combined. Scrape pancake mixture onto the baking sheet and spread evenly with a spatula.

**3.** In a small bowl, combine brown sugar, melted butter, and cinnamon. Scrape into a small resealable plastic bag.

**4.** Arrange banana pieces in upper-left quadrant of pancake. Sprinkle chocolate chips in upper-right quadrant and top with strawberries. In lower-right quadrant, pipe cinnamon-sugar mixture in swirls. Arrange blueberries in lower-left quadrant.

**5.** Bake until pancake is puffed and pulls from edges of pan, 14 to 16 minutes. Switch oven to broil and broil until golden, about 2 minutes.

**6.** In a small bowl, microwave peanut butter until melted and drizzle over banana in upper-left quadrant. Sprinkle lemon zest over blueberries.

**7.** Slice, and serve with maple syrup.

# Chapter 2

## SNACKS

It's always "let's eat" o'clock.

# Apple Chips

Serves 2 • Total Time: 3 hours

BEGINNER     PRO-IN-TRAINING     PRO

To the left, potatoes. There's a new chip in town! Don't worry if these are not crunchy right out of the oven—they'll crisp up as they cool.

| Ingredients | Amount |
| --- | --- |
| Apples | 2, thinly sliced |
| Granulated sugar | 2 teaspoons |
| Ground cinnamon | ½ teaspoon |

1. Preheat oven to 200°F. In a large bowl, toss apples with sugar and cinnamon using your hands.

2. Place a metal rack on a rimmed baking sheet. Lay apples slices on top of rack, spacing them so that no apples overlap.

3. Bake for 2 to 3 hours, flipping apples halfway through with tongs, until apples are dried out but still pliable.

4. Let cool on baking sheets. (Apples will continue to crisp while cooling.)

**What You'll Need**

Large Bowl

Metal Rack

Rimmed Baking Sheet

Tongs

Oven Mitts

**Warning!**
Have a grown-up help cut thin slices.

# English Muffin Pizzas

**Serves 6 • Total Time: 25 minutes**

BEGINNER    PRO-IN-TRAINING    PRO

This is the easiest and fastest way to satisfy your pizza craving. Plus, those famous English muffin nooks and crannies are perfect for catching sauce and melty cheese.

| Ingredients | Amount |
| --- | --- |
| English muffins | 6, split in half |
| Extra-virgin olive oil | |
| Garlic powder | 1½ teaspoons |
| Pizza sauce | ¾ cup |
| Grated Parmesan | ¼ cup |
| Fresh mozzarella | About 4 ounces, torn into pieces |
| Mini pepperoni | Optional |
| Torn fresh basil | Optional |

No need to measure! Just drizzle straight from the bottle.

**1.** Preheat oven to 400°F. Place English muffins on a large baking sheet, drizzle with oil, and sprinkle with garlic powder. Bake until tops are toasty, about 10 minutes.

**2.** Spoon a tablespoon of sauce onto the top of each half and spread in an even layer. Sprinkle with Parmesan and place mozzarella pieces on top. Top with pepperoni, if using.

**3.** Bake 10 minutes, until cheese is melty. Top with basil, if using, and serve.

**What You'll Need**

Large Baking Sheet

Spoon

Oven Mitts

# Oatmeal Chocolate Chip Balls

**Makes 30 • Total Time: 40 minutes**

BEGINNER     PRO-IN-TRAINING     PRO

Think of these as a cross between a chewy granola bar and an oatmeal chocolate chip cookie. Bonus: They're secretly healthy.

### What You'll Need

Large Baking Sheet

Parchment Paper

Large Bowl

Spatula

| Ingredients | Amount |
| --- | --- |
| Old-fashioned rolled oats | ⅔ cup |
| Unsweetened shredded coconut | ¼ cup |
| Mini chocolate chips | 2 tablespoons |
| Chia seeds | 1 tablespoon |
| Ground flaxseeds | 1 tablespoon |
| Ground cinnamon | ¼ teaspoon |
| Kosher salt | Pinch |
| Natural peanut butter | ⅓ cup |
| Honey | 2 tablespoons |
| Pure vanilla extract | ¼ teaspoon |
| Milk (any kind) | 1 to 2 tablespoons |

A good-for-you ingredient found in all sorts of foods, like crackers and waffles. Here, it's used instead of flour!

**1.** Line a large baking sheet with parchment paper. In a large bowl, combine oats, coconut, chocolate chips, chia, flax, cinnamon, and salt. Stir in peanut butter, honey, vanilla, and 1 tablespoon milk. Mixture should be slightly crumbly. If it's too dry, gradually stir in up to 1 more tablespoon of milk.

**2.** With wet hands, roll mixture into small balls and place onto baking sheet. Refrigerate until chilled, 30 minutes.

# Puppy Chow

**Serves 10 to 12 • Total Time: 15 minutes**

━━●━━━━━━━━━━━━━━━━━━━━━━━

BEGINNER       PRO-IN-TRAINING       PRO

People call this sweet snack by many different names: puppy chow, monkey munch, and muddy buddies. No matter what you call it, it's just about impossible to stop eating once you start.

## What You'll Need

Medium Microwave-Safe Bowl

Wooden Spoon

Large Bowl

Large Resealable Plastic Bag

Large Baking Sheet

Oven Mitts

| Ingredients | Amount |
| --- | --- |
| Semisweet chocolate chips | 1 cup |
| Peanut butter | ⅔ cup |
| Butter | ¼ cup (½ stick) |
| Pure vanilla extract | 1 teaspoon |
| Kosher salt | ½ teaspoon |
| Rice Chex cereal | 10 cups |
| Powdered sugar | 2 cups, plus more if needed |

**1.** Combine chocolate chips, peanut butter, and butter in a medium microwave–safe bowl. Microwave on high for 1 minute, then stir with wooden spoon to combine. Continue microwaving in 20–second increments until mixture is completely melty. Add vanilla and salt and stir until smooth.

**2.** Pour cereal into a large bowl, then pour chocolate mixture over cereal. Toss gently with wooden spoon until all cereal is coated.

**3.** Transfer chocolate–coated cereal to a large resealable plastic bag, then add powdered sugar and shake to coat. Pour cereal onto a large baking sheet to cool, 10 minutes. Serve immediately, or store in an airtight container until ready to serve.

**FYI!**
The bowl will be hot, so be careful and use an oven mitt!

37

# Cool Ranch Chickpeas

**Serves 6 • Total Time: 55 minutes**

BEGINNER     PRO-IN-TRAINING     PRO

Chances are high that you have a can of chickpeas somewhere in the house. A little time in the oven (and some ranch seasoning) and they become the most irresistible snack ever.

| Ingredients | Amount |
| --- | --- |
| Chickpeas | 2 (15-ounce) cans, drained and rinsed |
| Extra-virgin olive oil | ½ cup |
| Ranch seasoning | 2 tablespoons |

**1.** Preheat oven to 400°F and dry chickpeas very well with paper towels. Spread out chickpeas on a large baking sheet in an even layer. Bake until golden and crisp, 30 minutes.

**2.** Carefully transfer hot chickpeas to a large bowl. Using a spatula, toss chickpeas with oil and ranch seasoning. Spread out again on the baking sheet and bake for 5 minutes more.

**3.** Let chickpeas cool on the baking sheet.

## What You'll Need

Paper Towels

Large Baking Sheet

Large Bowl

Spatula

Oven Mitts

What's the difference between a chickpea and a garbanzo bean? Nothing!

## Cooking With Grandma

Try Champa's cozy drink recipe!

Champa Sheladia learned to cook when she was 12 years old while watching her grandmother in the kitchen in Ahmedabad, India. "In a way, I taught myself how to cook!" she exclaims proudly. Today she focuses on good-for-you homestyle Gujarati recipes with "a veggie-forward mindset." (Gujarat is a state on the western coast of India.)

The biggest lesson she was taught in the kitchen is never to waste food. "There's always a way to reuse leftovers," she says.

**What You'll Need**

Small Saucepan

Wooden Spoon

# Haldar nu Doodh

**Serves 2 • Total Time: 10 minutes**

BEGINNER     PRO-IN-TRAINING     PRO

Pronounced *hul–DUR nu DHOO–dh* this warm turmeric drink is extra comforting on a cold day or whenever you're feeling under the weather.

| Ingredients | Amount |
| --- | --- |
| Milk | 2 cups |
| Ground cardamom | ¼ teaspoon |
| Turmeric powder | ¼ teaspoon |
| Saffron | 4 to 5 strands, optional |
| Freshly ground black pepper | Pinch |
| Honey | To taste |

**1.** Heat milk in a small saucepan over medium heat. Add cardamom, turmeric, saffron, and black pepper.

**2.** Stir constantly until milk begins to bubble and steam. Remove from heat.

**3.** Pour into mugs and sweeten with honey to taste.

It's expensive, and a little bit goes a long way. Use it sparingly!

41

# Sour Patch Grapes

**Serves 10 • Total Time: 10 minutes**

BEGINNER      PRO-IN-TRAINING      PRO

BELIEVE IT. This magical recipe transforms green grapes into a sweet-and-sour snack that tastes suspiciously like Sour Patch Kids.

| Ingredients | Amount |
| --- | --- |
| Strawberry Jell-O | 1 (3-ounce) package |
| Orange Jell-O | 1 (3-ounce) package |
| Lemon Jell-O | 1 (3-ounce) package |
| Lime Jell-O | 1 (3-ounce) package |
| Green grapes | 1½ pounds |
| Lemon | ½ |

**1.** Empty each Jell-O packet into its own gallon-size resealable plastic bag.

**2.** Remove grapes from stems and rinse in a colander, shaking the colander to remove any excess water (grapes should be damp, not dripping wet). Squeeze lemon juice over grapes and toss with your hands so that all the grapes get lightly coated.

**3.** Place a handful of grapes in each bag of Jell-O mix, seal, then shake to coat.

**4.** Remove from resealable bags and serve.

**What You'll Need**

Large Resealable Plastic Bags

Colander

# California Sushi Bites

**Serves 6 • Total Time: 15 minutes**

BEGINNER    PRO-IN-TRAINING    PRO

This crunchy cucumber snack is inspired by a popular, but not traditional, type of sushi. In fact, when people from Japan talk about sushi, they're usually referring to nigiri sushi—thin slices of fresh raw fish served atop pillows of rice.

| Ingredients | Amount |
| --- | --- |
| Lemon | 1, halved |
| Avocado | 1, mashed or sliced |
| Kosher salt | |
| Freshly ground black pepper | |
| Large cucumber | 1, sliced into ¼-inch coins |
| Lump crabmeat | 8 ounces |
| Mayonnaise | ½ cup |
| Sriracha | 2 teaspoons, optional |
| Green onions | 3, thinly sliced, plus more for topping |
| Sesame seeds | For topping |
| Soy sauce | For serving |

**1.** In a medium bowl, squeeze lemon juice over avocado and season with salt and pepper. Use a fork to top each cucumber slice with avocado.

**2.** In another medium bowl, combine crabmeat, mayonnaise, Sriracha (if using), and green onions. Season with salt and pepper and stir with fork.

**3.** Top each cucumber slice with a small scoop of the crab mixture, then sprinkle with sesame seeds. Serve with soy sauce.

**What You'll Need**

2 Medium Bowls

Fork

# Types of Sushi

Get to know four common varieties.

### Nigiri

Slices of raw fish or vegetables draped over seasoned sushi rice

. . . . . . . . . . . . . . . . . . . . . . . . . . .

### Temaki

A hand-rolled cone of seaweed wrapped around rice and fillings

. . . . . . . . . . . . . . . . . . . . . . . . . . .

### Maki

Fish, meat, and/or vegetables rolled up inside nori (seaweed) with seasoned sushi rice

. . . . . . . . . . . . . . . . . . . . . . . . . . .

### Uramaki

An inside-out maki roll with rice on the outside

## A True Tale of Sushi

Historians believe that sushi was introduced to Japan in the 9th century (that's more than 1,000 years ago). But the dish was very different: Fish were caught and packed in salted rice, then weighed down for at least six months to ferment (a process used to preserve foods) before eating. In the 1820s, a man named Hanaya Yohei invented a type of sushi (nigiri) we know today. In the mid-1960s, Kawafuku, the first real sushi bar in the United States, opened in Los Angeles.

# Cinnamon Sugar Chips

**Serves 6 • Total Time: 30 minutes**

**BEGINNER**  •  **PRO-IN-TRAINING**  •  **PRO**

If you love flour tortillas, you're gonna fall in love with these cinnamon sugar chips. Be sure to keep an eye on them while baking—these babies crisp up fast.

| Ingredients | Amount |
| --- | --- |
| Medium flour tortillas | 6 |
| Melted butter | 4 tablespoons |
| Granulated sugar | 1 cup |
| Ground cinnamon | 1½ tablespoons |

1. Preheat oven to 425°F. Cut each tortilla into 8 triangles and arrange on a large baking sheet. Drizzle melted butter over cut tortillas, then mix together using your hands. Make sure both sides of each triangle are coated in butter!

2. In a medium bowl, use a fork to mix together cinnamon and sugar. Working with a handful of tortillas at a time, toss tortillas in cinnamon sugar.

3. Return cinnamon-sugar-coated tortillas to the baking sheet in a single layer.

4. Bake until crispy, 8 to 10 minutes. Let cool on pan 5 minutes before serving.

**What You'll Need**

Large Baking Sheet

Fork

Medium Bowl

Chef's Knife

Oven Mitts

This recipe works in an air fryer too! Working in batches, place tortillas in air-fryer basket in a single layer. Cook at 375°F for 6 minutes.

# Zucchini Tots

**Serves 4 • Total Time: 30 minutes**

BEGINNER     PRO-IN-TRAINING     PRO

A tater tot doesn't have to be made of taters. Zucchini and cheddar make these almost better than the classic.

| Ingredients | Amount |
| --- | --- |
| Cooking spray | For pan |
| Large zucchini | 3 |
| Large eggs | 2 |
| Shredded cheddar | ½ cup |
| Grated Parmesan | ½ cup |
| Dried oregano | 1 teaspoon |
| Garlic powder | ¼ teaspoon |
| Kosher salt | ½ teaspoon |
| Freshly ground black pepper | |
| Ketchup | For serving |

**What You'll Need**

Baking Sheet

Box Grater

Kitchen Towel

Large Bowl

Whisk

Oven Mitts

**1.** Preheat oven to 400°F and grease a baking sheet with cooking spray. Using a box grater, grate zucchini onto a clean kitchen towel. Gather ends of the kitchen towel to cover zucchini completely, then squeeze out excess liquid over sink.

**2.** In a large bowl, whisk eggs until yolks are broken up and mixture is yellow. Add zucchini, cheddar, Parmesan, oregano, garlic powder, salt, and pepper and mix until combined. Scoop 1 tablespoon of mixture and roll it into a tater-tot shape with your hands. Place on the baking sheet.

**3.** Bake until golden, 15 to 20 minutes. Serve with ketchup.

# 4-Way Dip

**Serves 4 • Total Time: 40 minutes**

BEGINNER ———●——— PRO-IN-TRAINING ——— PRO

This genius snack is a guaranteed touchdown.

| Ingredients | Amount |
|---|---|
| **For the biscuit dippers & base dip** | |
| Cooking spray | For pan |
| Refrigerated biscuits | 2 (16.3-ounce) cans |
| Melted butter | 4 tablespoons |
| Garlic powder | ½ teaspoon |
| Freshly grated Parmesan | ⅓ cup |
| Cream cheese | 3 (8-ounce) blocks, softened |
| Shredded mozzarella | 6 cups |
| **For Buffalo Chicken Dip** | |
| Shredded cooked chicken | 1½ cups |
| Buffalo sauce | ¼ cup |
| Ranch dressing | 1 tablespoon |
| Blue cheese crumbles | For topping |
| Freshly chopped chives | For topping |
| **For Spinach-Artichoke Dip** | |
| Baby spinach | ¾ cup |
| Sour cream | ⅓ cup |
| Artichoke hearts | ½ cup, chopped |
| **For Jalapeño Popper Dip** | |
| Cooked bacon | 4 slices, crumbled |
| Sour cream | ⅓ cup |
| Jalapeños | 2, minced |
| **For Pizza Dip** | |
| Pizza sauce | ½ cup |
| Shredded mozzarella | ¼ cup |
| Mini pepperoni | ¼ cup |
| Italian seasoning | 1 teaspoon |
| Torn fresh basil | For topping |

## What You'll Need

- Large Baking Sheet
- Paring Knife
- Pastry Brush
- Large Bowl
- Mixer
- 2 Medium Bowls
- Spatula
- Oven Mitts

Jalapeño Popper Dip

Spinach-Artichoke Dip

Pizza Dip

Buffalo Chicken Dip

1. Preheat oven to 350°F and grease a large baking sheet with cooking spray.

2. **Make dippers:** Cut each biscuit into 4 pieces and pinch edges together to form a ball. Place biscuits around edges of prepared baking sheet and then in lengthwise and crosswise lines down the middle to create four separate quadrants.

3. Brush biscuits with melted butter and top with garlic powder and Parmesan.

4. **Make base dip:** In a large bowl using a hand mixer or in the bowl of a stand mixer, beat cream cheese and mozzarella until combined.

5. **Make Buffalo Chicken Dip:** Transfer about a quarter of the base dip to a medium bowl, then mix in chicken, Buffalo sauce, and ranch. Scrape into a quadrant with spatula.

6. **Make Spinach–Artichoke Dip:** Transfer another quarter of the base dip to a medium bowl, then stir in spinach, sour cream, and artichokes. Transfer to a quadrant.

7. **Make Pizza Dip:** Transfer another quarter of base dip to an empty quadrant. Spoon pizza sauce over dip, then sprinkle with more mozzarella, pepperoni, and Italian seasoning.

8. **Make Jalapeño Popper Dip:** Add sour cream, most of the bacon (save some for topping!), and jalapeños to remaining base dip and stir. Transfer to last quadrant.

9. Bake until biscuits are golden and cheese is melty, 30 minutes.

10. Top Buffalo Chicken Dip with blue cheese and chives. Top Spinach–Artichoke Dip with parsley. Top Jalapeño Popper Dip with remaining bacon crumbles. Top Pizza Dip with basil.

51

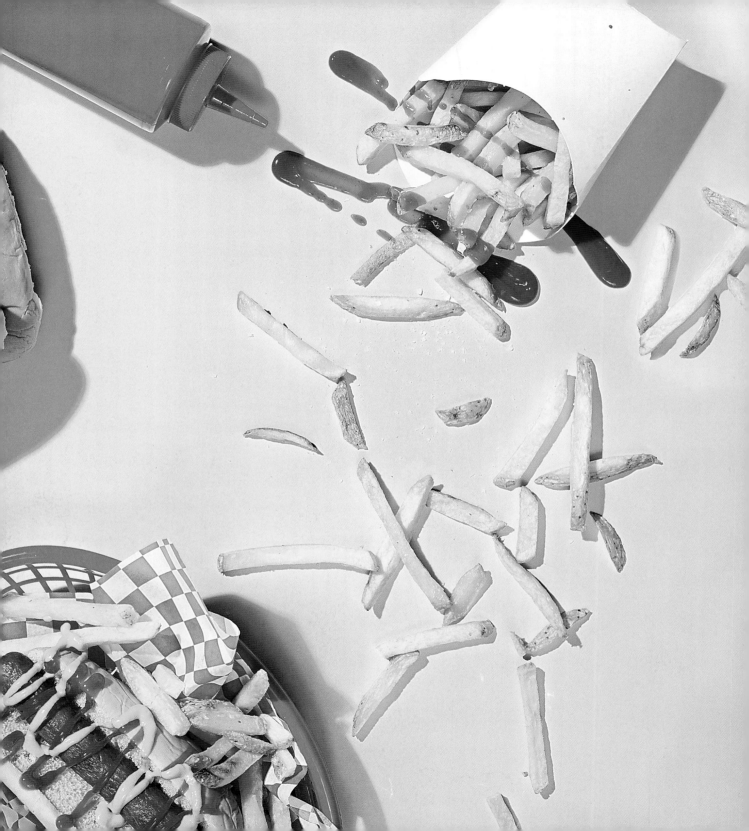

# Chapter 3

# Lunchtime!

Treat yourself to a
midday feast!

# Big Mac Quesadillas

Serves 4 • Total Time: 40 minutes

BEGINNER    PRO-IN-TRAINING    PRO

Switch up your lunch game with something over-the-top and McDonald's-inspired. This recipe makes just enough special sauce to drizzle inside the quesadillas. Feel free to double it if you want more for dipping!

| Ingredients | Amount |
| --- | --- |
| **For the special sauce** | |
| **Mayonnaise** | ¾ cup |
| **Yellow mustard** | 3 tablespoons |
| **Ketchup** | 1 tablespoon |
| **Pickle relish** | 1 tablespoon |
| **Apple cider vinegar** | 2 teaspoons |
| **Garlic powder** | ½ teaspoon |
| **Onion powder** | ½ teaspoon |
| **Sweet paprika** | ¼ teaspoon |
| **Kosher salt** | |
| **For the quesadillas** | |
| **Extra-virgin olive oil** | 1 tablespoon |
| **Ground beef** | ½ pound |
| **Kosher salt** | |
| **Freshly ground black pepper** | |
| **Cooking spray** | For pan |
| **Medium flour tortillas** | 4 |
| **American cheese** | 4 slices |
| **Shredded cheddar** | 1 cup |
| **White onion** | ¼, chopped |
| **Sliced bread-and-butter pickles** | For serving |

This has a strong smell but helps brighten the flavor of the creamy, sweet sauce.

**What You'll Need**

Small Bowl

Spoon

Nonstick Skillet

Wooden Spoon

Slotted Spoon

Plate

Paper Towels

**1. Make special sauce:** In a small bowl, use a spoon to stir together all sauce ingredients until well combined.

**2. Cook beef:** In a large nonstick pan over medium–high heat, heat oil. When oil is shimmering, add ground beef and season with salt and pepper. Cook, breaking up meat with a wooden spoon, until beef is cooked through and no longer pink, 6 minutes. Using a slotted spoon, transfer the ground beef to a plate. Drain excess fat from skillet and wipe clean with paper towels.

**3. Make quesadillas:** Place skillet over medium heat and grease with cooking spray. Add a flour tortilla, and top half of the tortilla with ½ slice American cheese, ¼ cup cheddar, and a generous spoonful of ground beef. Sprinkle with some onion. Drizzle with special sauce and top with another ½ slice American cheese. Fold the untopped half over the cheese and beef, and cook until deeply golden, about 1 minute. Flip quesadilla and cook 1 to 2 minutes more, until golden on the other side.

**4.** Repeat with remaining ingredients to make three more quesadillas.

**5.** Slice into triangles, and top with pickles.

If you don't have a waffle maker, you can cook the sandwiches in a nonstick pan over medium heat. It'll take about 2 minutes for the first side and 1 minute for the second side.

# Waffle Iron Grilled Cheese

**Serves 2 • Total Time: 15 minutes**

BEGINNER          PRO-IN-TRAINING          PRO

## What You'll Need

Fork

Small Bowl

Butter Knife

Waffle Iron

People who are pros at grilled cheese always debate: Should you put mayo or butter on the bread? Here's our take: Mayo is easily spreadable and gives you a uniformly golden and crisp grilled cheese. But butter tastes better. The solution: Use both!

| Ingredients | Amount |
| --- | --- |
| Mayonnaise | 1 tablespoon |
| Butter | 1 tablespoon, softened |
| Sourdough bread | 4 slices |
| American cheese | 2 slices |
| Shredded Monterey jack | ¾ cup |
| Shredded cheddar | ¾ cup |
| Cooking spray | For waffle iron |

**Warning!** Ask a parent for help! With the exception of the handles and knobs, the whole waffle iron will get super hot.

**1.** In a small bowl, mix mayonnaise and butter with a fork. Arrange the bread in a single layer on a work surface. Spread mayonnaise mixture onto the top side of each slice with a butter knife. Flip two slices of bread, so they're mayonnaise side down, then top each of these with a slice of American cheese, half the Monterey jack, and half the cheddar. Top with the remaining slice of bread, mayonnaise side up.

**2.** Heat waffle iron to medium heat. Grease waffle iron with cooking spray, then carefully add one sandwich. Close waffle iron, and cook until cheese is melted and bread is golden, about 3 minutes. Remove carefully and repeat with the remaining sandwich.

# Fun Things to Make With
# Chicken Nuggets

BEGINNER      PRO-IN-TRAINING      PRO

It's hard to beat freshly baked chicken nuggets
straight from the oven, but if you're ready
to graduate from a simple ketchup or barbecue
dipping sauce, try one of these fun and
crazy–easy makeovers.

## Sliders
**Hawaiian rolls**
**+ Lettuce**
**+ Tomato**
**+ Mayo**

## Buffalo Chicken Wraps
**Tortilla**
**+ Melted butter**
**+ Frank's RedHot sauce**
**+ Chopped celery**
**+ Ranch**

## Chicken, Bacon, Ranch, Lettuce Cups
**Butterhead lettuce**
**+ Bacon**
**+ Tomatoes**
**+ Ranch**

**Tacos**

Hard taco shells
+ Shredded cheese
+ Pico de gallo
+ Guacamole
+ Sour cream

**Chicken & Waffle Cone**

Waffle cone
+ Oven fries
+ Maple syrup

**Cobb Salad**

Romaine
+ Chopped tomatoes
+ Diced avocado
+ Bacon
+ Blue cheese
+ Your favorite bottled dressing

59

# Hot Dog Cubanos

**Serves 4 • Total Time: 40 minutes**

BEGINNER     PRO-IN-TRAINING     PRO

This twist on a Cubano swaps in sliced hot dogs for the roasted pork and we're not mad about this definitely-not-traditional substitution. (It's hard to be mad at a hot dog.)

| Ingredients | Amount |
| --- | --- |
| Hot dogs | 6 |
| Black Forest ham | 6 slices |
| Cuban bread or hero rolls | 2 loaves, split lengthwise |
| Yellow mustard | ¼ cup |
| Swiss cheese | 4 slices, halved |
| Dill pickles | 6 slices |
| Butter | 2 tablespoons, softened |

**1.** Using a paring knife, slice each hot dog in half lengthwise (to make two long, skinnier pieces).

**2.** Heat a cast-iron skillet over medium-high heat. Add hot dogs and ham and cook, turning once with tongs, until lightly charred and warmed through, 4 minutes for the hot dogs and 1 minute for the ham. Remove to a plate.

**3.** Place rolls on a work surface, open sides up, and spread both halves with mustard and top with Swiss cheese. Add hot dogs, pickles, and ham to the bottom half of each sandwich. Close sandwiches and press gently. Spread butter all over the outside of the rolls with the butter knife.

**4.** Place sandwiches in hot skillet, then place another cast-iron skillet on top to weigh the sandwiches down. Cook until golden, 2 minutes. Remove top skillet, flip sandwiches, and cook until the other side is golden and cheese is melted, 2 minutes more.

**5.** Slice in half and serve.

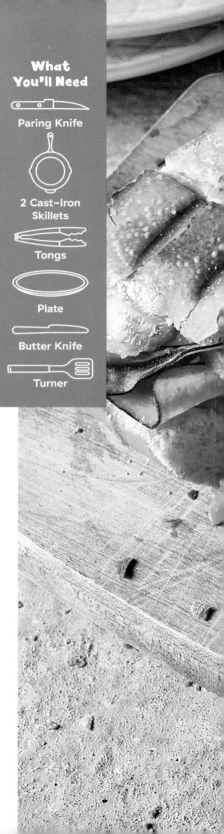

## What You'll Need

Paring Knife

2 Cast-Iron Skillets

Tongs

Plate

Butter Knife

Turner

## Did You Know?

A Cuban sandwich (aka Cubano) is the best possible version of a ham and cheese sandwich. It has layers of roasted pork, ham, Swiss cheese, pickles, and mustard and is pressed like a panini.

Whether the sandwich was invented in the United States or Cuba is unclear. What we know is that it became popular in Florida during the rise of the tobacco industry in the 1800s as a quick and affordable lunch for Cuban immigrants.

Tampa and Miami have a major rivalry over which is home to the best Cubano. In Tampa, where there is a large Italian population, the sandwiches are served with Genoa salami.

# Build-Your-Own Grain Bowl

**Serves 1 • Total Time: 25 minutes**

BEGINNER　　　PRO-IN-TRAINING　　　PRO

Just because it's healthy doesn't mean it's not extremely delicious. Mix and match the toppings all you want—there are no rules!

½ avocado, sliced

½ cup shredded rotisserie chicken

**1**

**Choose your base.** Add cooked grains to a bowl that's big enough to mix stuff in but not so big that it's unwieldy to eat out of.

1 cup cooked rice

1 cup cooked quinoa

1 cup cooked farro

**2**

**Add some protein.** Choose one or two and add to the bowl on top of grains.

1 hard-boiled egg, peeled and chopped

¼ cup canned chickpeas, drained and rinsed

**3**

**Pick your toppings.** Here's where you go crazy and try your own fun flavor combinations. Add as little or as much as you want—just eyeball it!

Ours has chicken, corn, lettuce, bacon, cheese, avocado, Fritos, and Ranch!

**Crushed pita chips**

**Shredded lettuce**

**Shredded cheddar**

**Sliced apples**

**Cooked bacon**

**Crushed Fritos**

**Chopped bell peppers**

**Crumbled goat cheese**

**Sliced cucumber**

**Chopped tomatoes**

**Corn kernels**

**Matchstick carrots**

Ranch

Thousand Island

**4**

**Dress it up.** Drizzle your favorite bottled dressing, mix everything up, and voilà! You've got a grain bowl.

Honey mustard

Balsamic

Italian

# Summer Rolls

Serves 8 • Total Time: 15 minutes

BEGINNER      PRO-IN-TRAINING      PRO

This traditional no-cook Vietnamese dish is filled with crunchy veggies, rice vermicelli (super-skinny rice noodles), and shrimp and encased in rice-paper sheets (super-thin wrappers that can be stuffed with almost anything).

| Ingredients | Amount |
| --- | --- |
| Rice vermicelli noodles | 3 ounces |
| Matchstick carrots | 1 cup |
| Persian cucumbers | 2, thinly sliced |
| Napa cabbage | 8 ounces, thinly sliced |
| Fish sauce | 1 tablespoon |
| Brown sugar | 1 tablespoon |
| Rice vinegar | ¼ cup |
| Large rice-paper sheets | 8 |
| Fresh mint leaves | 12 |
| Fresh basil leaves | 12 |
| Large cooked shrimp | 12, halved |
| Black sesame seeds | 2 tablespoons |

You can buy these precut from the grocery store!

What You'll Need

Medium Heatproof Bowl

Colander

Kitchen Scissors

Medium Bowl

Tongs

Kitchen Towel

Cutting Board

Small Bowl

Whisk

Microplane

1. Place noodles in a medium heatproof bowl and cover with boiling water; let stand about 5 minutes or until just tender, then drain into a colander. Using kitchen scissors, cut noodles into smaller pieces. (They don't need to be the same size!)

2. In the same bowl, mix noodles, carrots, cucumbers, cabbage, fish sauce, sugar, and vinegar; toss together gently with tongs.

3. To assemble rolls, place a sheet of rice paper in a medium bowl of warm water until just softened; lift sheet carefully from water and place it on a kitchen-towel-covered cutting board with a corner point facing toward you. Place some of the vegetable filling horizontally in center of sheet, top with 1 mint leaf, 1 basil leaf, 3 shrimp halves, and sesame seeds. Fold corner point facing you up over filling; roll sheet to enclose filling, folding in sides after first complete turn of roll. Repeat with remaining sheets.

## Fish Sauce

If you like pad Thai, you're already a fan. It's made from fermented fish, but it won't make your dish taste fishy—we promise! It is salty and sweet and can make almost anything taste better. You can find bottles of it in most supermarkets.

## Don't Forget the Peanut Sauce

Use a Microplane to grate 1 clove **garlic** and a 2-inch piece of peeled **ginger,** and add to small bowl. Add ½ cup **smooth peanut butter**, 1 tablespoon **soy sauce**, 2 tablespoons **rice vinegar**, and ¼ cup hot **water**, and whisk until smooth. Top with ¼ cup crushed **peanuts** and sprinkle with a pinch of **sesame seeds**. Serve with rolls as a dipping sauce.

# Chorizo Tacos

**Serves 4 • Total Time: 45 minutes**

BEGINNER      PRO-IN-TRAINING      PRO

Inspired loosely by tacos al pastor, this is a fun and easy meal that the whole family will request often.

| Ingredients | Amount |
| --- | --- |
| Finely chopped pineapple | 1 cup |
| Small white onion | ¼, finely chopped |
| Chopped cilantro | ¼ cup |
| Kosher salt | |
| Lime | ½ |
| Mexican chorizo | 1 pound |
| Extra-virgin olive oil | 1 tablespoon |
| Small corn tortillas | 8 |

If you're using canned pineapple, use tidbits!

**1. Make salsa:** In a medium bowl, use a spoon to mix together pineapple, onion, cilantro, and a pinch of salt. Squeeze lime juice over mixture and toss until combined.

**2. Cook chorizo:** Get a grown-up to help you cut a slit with a paring knife into each link of chorizo and remove the casing.

**3.** In a medium skillet over medium-high heat, heat oil. When oil is shimmering, add chorizo and use a wooden spoon to break up meat into large crumbles. Cook, stirring occasionally, until cooked through, 8 minutes.

**4. Warm tortillas:** Crumple 2 paper towels into 2 balls, then place each under running water for 2 seconds. Squeeze out excess water.

**5.** On a large microwave-safe plate, create 2 stacks of 4 tortillas, and cover each stack with 1 damp paper towel. Microwave in 30-second intervals until tortillas are warmed through, 1 minute 30 seconds.

**6. Assemble tacos:** Divide cooked chorizo among warm tortillas and top each with pineapple salsa.

## What You'll Need

Medium Bowl

Spoon

Paring Knife

Medium Skillet

Wooden Spoon

Paper Towels

Microwave-Safe Plate

# The Super-Fun History of
# TACOS

Food historians cannot tell you when the first-ever taco was made, but the food can be traced to the 18th century. **In Mexico, silver miners used the word "taco" to describe pieces of paper wrapped around gunpowder, used as explosives for digging.** Those miners are said to have coined the same nickname for their lunches, which were the same shape: tortillas wrapped around simple fillings. Mexico City became a hub of industrial jobs, and people from all over the country brought their regional taco recipes with them. Today, the city is still famous for its many taquerias, with locals and tourists alike debating the best spot.

**Many Mexican people came to California and Texas in the early 1900s to build railroads.** The tacos came with them, but the ingredients shifted to include ground beef, cheddar, iceberg lettuce, and tomato—foods more readily available in the United States. Texans lay claim to inventing the breakfast taco, commonly stuffed with eggs, cheese, and salsa.

California

Texas

Mexico

**Traditionally, tacos are filled with meat, fish, and/or veggies wrapped in either corn or flour tortillas.** Among the popular varieties are carnitas (pulled pork), pescado (fried fish), and nopales (cactus). Tacos al pastor, a roast pork and pineapple version, was inspired by shawarma, a Middle Eastern dish consisting of thinly sliced meat stacked into a conical shape that roasts slowly on a vertical spit. But these days, you can find a taco shell filled with just about anything—including scoops of ice cream and swirls of spaghetti!

Menu

Pollo
Carne Asada
Carnitas
Pescado
Nopales

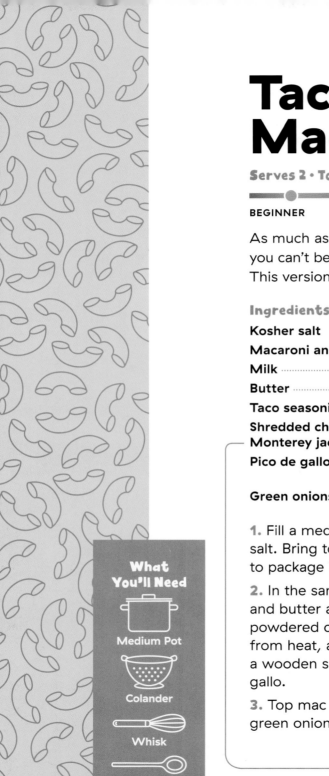

# Taco Mac & Cheese

**Serves 2 • Total Time: 25 minutes**

BEGINNER    PRO-IN-TRAINING    PRO

As much as we love a good homemade mac, you can't beat the convenience of the boxed variety. This version takes it up a few levels.

| Ingredients | Amount |
| --- | --- |
| Kosher salt | |
| Macaroni and cheese | 1 (7.25–ounce) box |
| Milk | ¼ cup |
| Butter | 2 tablespoons |
| Taco seasoning | ½ teaspoon |
| Shredded cheddar or Monterey jack | ½ cup |
| Pico de gallo | ½ cup, drained, plus more for serving |
| Green onions | 2, thinly sliced |

**1.** Fill a medium pot with water and add a big pinch of salt. Bring to a boil over high heat. Cook pasta according to package instructions, then drain into a colander.

**2.** In the same pot over medium–low heat, add milk and butter and whisk until butter is melted. Whisk in powdered cheese packet and taco seasoning. Remove from heat, add pasta and shredded cheese, and stir with a wooden spoon until cheese has melted. Stir in pico de gallo.

**3.** Top mac and cheese with more pico de gallo and green onions before serving.

**What You'll Need**

Medium Pot

Colander

Whisk

Wooden Spoon

Adding shredded cheese is a major game changer!

## Give It a Try

### Pico de Gallo

Also called salsa fresca, pico de gallo is a chunky, uncooked salsa commonly used in Mexican cooking. It's typically made from chopped tomatoes, onion, fresh chiles, lime juice, cilantro, and salt.

Chapter 4

COPYCATS
COPYCATS
COPYCATS
**COPYCATS**
COPYCATS
COPYCATS
COPYCATS

Learn to make your restaurant favorites at home.

# Breakfast Crunchwrap Supreme

**Serves 4 • Total Time: 1 hour**

BEGINNER — PRO-IN-TRAINING — PRO

Breakfast burritos are so last year. Go all in on breakfast crunchwraps, the absurd and incredible Taco Bell—inspired creation with layers of crispy hash browns, scrambled eggs, cheese, and bacon.

| Ingredients | Amount |
| --- | --- |
| **Frozen hash brown patties** | 4 |
| **For the sauce** | |
| Sour cream | ⅓ cup |
| Smoked paprika | ¼ teaspoon |
| Lime | ½ |
| Kosher salt | |
| Freshly ground black pepper | |
| **For the scrambled eggs** | |
| Large eggs | 5 |
| Milk | 1 tablespoon |
| Butter | 1 tablespoon |
| Finely chopped chives | 2 tablespoons |
| **For assembly** | |
| Large flour tortillas | 4 |
| Cooked bacon | 6 slices, chopped |
| Shredded cheddar | 1 cup |
| Shredded Monterey jack | 1 cup |
| Vegetable oil | For pan |
| Hot sauce | For serving, optional |

INSPIRED BY TACO BELL!

**What You'll Need**

- Baking Sheet
- Small Bowl
- Whisk
- Large Bowl
- Medium Nonstick Pan
- Spatula
- Butter Knife
- Chef's Knife

**1. Make hash browns and sauce:**
Bake frozen hash brown patties according to package instructions. Meanwhile, make sour cream sauce. In a small bowl, whisk together sour cream and paprika, then squeeze lime juice into mixture and season with salt and pepper.

**2. Make scrambled eggs:** In a large bowl, combine eggs and milk and whisk until frothy. In a medium nonstick pan, melt butter over medium heat. Pour egg mixture into the pan. Cook for 1 minute, then reduce heat to medium low. Drag the eggs with a spatula to create curds and cook until eggs are no longer runny, 3 minutes. Fold in chives and remove from heat.

**3. Assemble crunchwraps:** Spread the sour cream sauce onto the center of each flour tortilla with a butter knife, then top each with a hash brown patty, scrambled eggs, bacon, cheddar, and Monterey jack. Fold tortillas around the center, creating pleats. After wrapping, quickly invert crunchwraps so the pleats are on the bottom and they stay together.

**4. Cook crunchwraps:** In a medium nonstick pan over medium heat, heat a very thin layer of vegetable oil. Working one at a time, add crunchwrap seam side down and cook until tortilla is golden on the bottom, 2 to 4 minutes. Flip crunchwrap and cook until the other side is golden, 2 to 4 minutes more.

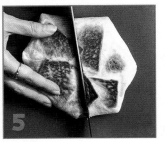

**5.** Repeat with remaining crunchwraps. Cut each in half and serve warm.

# Leprechaun Shake

**Makes 1 • Total Time: 5 minutes**

BEGINNER　　　PRO-IN-TRAINING　　　PRO

The first-ever McDonald's Shamrock Shake—first introduced nationally in 1970—wasn't mint flavored. It was lemon–lime, made with a combination of vanilla ice cream and lemon–lime sherbet. We're in favor of the modern version, flavored with peppermint extract.

| Ingredients | Amount |
| --- | --- |
| Vanilla ice cream | 3 large scoops (about ¼ cup each) |
| Heavy cream | ¼ cup |
| Peppermint extract | ½ teaspoon |
| Green food coloring | 6 drops |
| Whipped cream | For topping |
| Maraschino cherry | 1, for topping |

1. In a blender, mix vanilla ice cream, heavy cream, peppermint extract, and food coloring until completely smooth, then pour into a glass.

2. Top with whipped cream and a cherry before serving.

# Chicken Burrito Bowls

**Serves 4 • Total Time: 2 hours 20 minutes**

BEGINNER    PRO-IN-TRAINING    PRO

INSPIRED BY CHIPOTLE!

No need to wait in line when you can make killer Chipotle–style burrito bowls at home. Load yours up with any and every possible topping—especially guac, because it isn't extra.

| Ingredients | Amount |
| --- | --- |
| **For the chicken** | |
| Medium red onion | ½, roughly chopped |
| Garlic | 2 cloves |
| Chipotle pepper in adobo sauce | 1, plus 2 tablespoons sauce |
| Vegetable oil | 3 tablespoons |
| Dried oregano | 1 teaspoon |
| Ground cumin | ½ teaspoon |
| Kosher salt | |
| Freshly ground black pepper | |
| Boneless skinless chicken breasts | 1 pound |
| **For serving** | |
| Cooked rice | 2 cups |
| Corn | ½ cup |
| Black beans | ½ cup, drained and rinsed |
| Guacamole | ½ cup |
| Salsa | ½ cup |
| Lime wedges | 4 |

**What You'll Need**

Food Processor

Large Resealable Plastic Bag

Grill Pan or Cast-Iron Skillet

Tongs

Chef's Knife

1. **Make marinade:** In a food processor, blend onion, garlic, chipotle pepper and adobo sauce, oil, oregano, and cumin until smooth. Season with salt and pepper.

2. Add marinade and chicken to a large resealable plastic bag and rub all over to coat chicken. Let marinate in the fridge for at least 2 hours.

3. **Cook chicken:** Bring chicken to room temperature and preheat grill pan (or cast–iron skillet) to high. Grill chicken until cooked through, about 4 minutes per side. Let rest 10 minutes before carefully slicing into strips.

4. Divide rice, corn, black beans, guacamole, salsa, and lime wedges among 4 bowls and top with sliced chicken.

# BBQ Chicken Pizza

**Makes 2 • Total Time: 45 minutes**

BEGINNER        PRO-IN-TRAINING        PRO

INSPIRED BY CALIFORNIA PIZZA KITCHEN!

There's something about California Pizza Kitchen's trademark pizza that's irresistible. On paper, it doesn't sound like it would work. But on dough, it totally does.

## What You'll Need

2 Large Baking Sheets

Medium Bowl

Rolling Pin

Oven Mitts

| Ingredients | Amount |
| --- | --- |
| Cooking spray | For pan |
| Cooked shredded chicken | 2 cups |
| Barbecue sauce | ¾ cup, divided |
| All-purpose flour | For surface |
| Refrigerated pizza dough | 1 pound, divided into 2 pieces |
| Shredded mozzarella | 1 cup |
| Medium red onion | ¼, thinly sliced |
| Shredded Gouda | ⅓ cup |
| Freshly chopped cilantro | 2 tablespoons |

**1.** Preheat oven to 500°F. Grease two large baking sheets with cooking spray. In a medium bowl, stir together chicken and ¼ cup barbecue sauce.

**2.** Sprinkle some flour onto a clean counter or work surface. Gently flatten each ball of dough and roll with a rolling pin (or stretch with your hands) until about 12 inches in diameter (or as thin as you can).

**3.** Top each pizza with ¼ cup barbecue sauce, then half the chicken mixture, spreading in an even layer and leaving a 1-inch border around the edge. Add an even layer of mozzarella and red onion, then top with Gouda.

**4.** Bake until cheese is melty and dough is golden and cooked through, 20 to 25 minutes. Top with cilantro before serving.

# Cheddar Biscuits

**Makes 16 • Total Time: 35 minutes**

BEGINNER · · · · · · · PRO-IN-TRAINING · · · · · · · PRO

Those in the know will tell you: The best item on Red Lobster's menu has nothing to do with seafood. These cheddar-laced, butter-drenched biscuits are so good, it's hard not to polish them off in one sitting.

INSPIRED BY RED LOBSTER!

## What You'll Need

Baking Sheet

Parchment Paper

Large Bowl

Mixer

Spatula

Spoon

Small Microwave-Safe Bowl

Oven Mitts

Basting Brush

| Ingredients | Amount |
|---|---|
| **For the biscuits** | |
| All-purpose flour | 3 cups |
| Baking powder | 2 tablespoons |
| Butter | ¾ cup (1½ sticks), cold, cut into small pieces |
| Kosher salt | ¼ teaspoon |
| Whole milk | 1¾ cups |
| Garlic powder | 2 teaspoons |
| Shredded cheddar | 1½ cups |
| **For the topping** | |
| Butter | ½ cup (1 stick) |
| Freshly chopped parsley | 1 tablespoon |
| Garlic powder | 1 teaspoon |

**1.** Preheat oven to 400°F and line a large baking sheet with parchment paper. To a large bowl or bowl of a stand mixer, add flour, baking powder, butter, and salt. Starting on low, use a hand mixer or a stand mixer to combine ingredients. Gradually work your way up to medium speed until you've formed a dough with pea-size lumps. Reduce mixer speed to low and slowly add in milk.

**2.** Use a spatula to fold in garlic powder and cheese. Use a spoon to place 2-inch pieces of dough onto baking sheet. Bake until lightly golden, 18 to 20 minutes.

**3.** In a small microwave-safe bowl, melt butter in 20-second intervals, stirring in between, until fully melted. Stir in parsley and garlic powder.

**4.** Brush mixture on top of each biscuit with basting brush as soon as they're out of the oven, and serve immediately.

# Famous Chocolate Chip Cookies

**Makes 2 dozen • Total Time: 30 minutes**

BEGINNER        PRO-IN-TRAINING        PRO

INSPIRED BY MRS. FIELDS!

Save yourself a "Fields" trip to the mall and make these iconic chocolate chip cookies at home.

| Ingredients | Amount |
| --- | --- |
| All-purpose flour | 2½ cups |
| Baking soda | 1 teaspoon |
| Kosher salt | ¾ teaspoon |
| Butter | 1 cup (2 sticks), cold, cut into cubes |
| Brown sugar | 1 cup, packed |
| Granulated sugar | ½ cup |
| Large eggs | 2 |
| Pure vanilla extract | 2 teaspoons |
| Semisweet chocolate chips | 2 cups |

**1.** Preheat oven to 350°F and line two large baking sheets with parchment paper. In a medium bowl, whisk together flour, baking soda, and salt.

**2.** In a large bowl using a hand mixer or in the bowl of a stand mixer, cream together butter and sugars until mixture resembles coarse sand. Add eggs and vanilla and beat until combined. Add dry ingredients and mix until just combined, then fold in chocolate chips with a spatula.

**3.** Using a medium cookie scoop, form dough into balls and place on baking sheets. Bake until golden, 13 to 15 minutes.

## What You'll Need

- 2 Large Baking Sheets
- Parchment Paper
- Medium Bowl
- Whisk
- Large Bowl
- Mixer
- Spatula
- Medium Cookie Scoop
- Oven Mitts

# Pineapple Whip

Serves 4 • Total Time: 10 minutes

BEGINNER     PRO-IN-TRAINING     PRO

INSPIRED BY WALT DISNEY WORLD!

This copycat frozen drink will make all your Disney dreams come true. Treat yourself to a glass of pure sunshine.

| Ingredients | Amount |
| --- | --- |
| Frozen pineapple chunks | 3 cups |
| Bananas | 2, peeled, sliced, frozen |
| Coconut milk | ¾ cup |
| Sweetened condensed milk | ¼ cup |
| Pineapple slices | For topping |
| Maraschino cherries | For topping |

**FYI!**
The mixture will be thick!

**1.** In a blender, pulse all ingredients except cherries until combined, then blend until smooth.

**2.** Pour into a resealable plastic bag, using a rubber spatula to scrape out every last bit. Seal bag, then snip off a corner with scissors.

**3.** Pipe into glasses and top with a piece of pineapple and a cherry.

## What You'll Need

Blender

Large Resealable Plastic Bag

Spatula

Make it strawberry flavored (and pink!) by subbing out the bananas for 3 cups quartered frozen strawberries.

# Secret Menu Cheeseburgers

**Makes 4 • Total Time: 1 hour**

BEGINNER · PRO-IN-TRAINING · PRO

Regardless of where your fast-food allegiances lie, there's no denying the beauty of the not-so-secret In-N-Out animal-style burger. The trick to recreating it at home: slathering the patties with yellow mustard before cooking.

| Ingredients | Amount |
| --- | --- |
| **For the onions** | |
| **Vegetable oil** | **1 tablespoon** |
| **Butter** | **1 tablespoon** |
| **Large onion** | **1, chopped** |
| **Kosher salt** | |
| **Freshly ground black pepper** | |
| **For the sauce** | |
| **Mayonnaise** | **½ cup** |
| **Ketchup** | **2 tablespoons** |
| **Sweet pickle relish** | **2 tablespoons** |
| **Granulated sugar** | **2 teaspoons** |
| **For the burgers** | |
| **Ground beef** | **¾ pound** |
| **Kosher salt** | |
| **Freshly ground black pepper** | |
| **Yellow mustard** | **4 tablespoons** |
| **American cheese** | **4 slices** |
| **Hamburger buns** | **4** |
| **Iceberg lettuce** | **4 leaves** |
| **Tomato** | **1, sliced** |

**What You'll Need**

- 2 Large Skillets
- Wooden Spoon
- Small Bowl
- Whisk
- Turner
- Spoon
- Butter Knife

The caramelized onions are part of what makes these burger "animal style," but feel free to skip them to save time. Slathering yellow mustard on the patties before cooking, on the other hand, is nonnegotiable.

**1. Caramelize onions:** In a large skillet over medium heat, heat oil with butter. Add onion and cook until it begins to sweat and turn golden, 5 minutes. Reduce heat to medium low and continue to cook until onion is very soft, 15 minutes more.

**2.** Add a splash of water to the pan, and scrape up any brown bits with a wooden spoon. Continue to cook until onions are jammy and caramel in color, adding a splash of water if onions start to dry out, 10 minutes. Season with salt and pepper.

**3. Make sauce:** In a small bowl, whisk together mayonnaise, ketchup, relish, and sugar.

**4. Make burgers:** Divide ground beef into 4 equal portions. Form meat into very thin patties (as thin as you can make them!). Season both sides with salt and pepper.

**5.** Heat a large skillet over medium–high heat. Add patties to skillet. With a turner, press down on patties to smash them even more. Spread a tablespoon of yellow mustard onto the raw side of each patty. When bottoms are seared and crusty, 4 minutes, flip patties.

**6.** Top each patty with a slice of cheese and cook until cheese is melty and burgers are cooked through, 4 minutes more. Repeat with remaining burgers. Spoon caramelized onions onto each cooked burger patty.

**7.** Spread sauce onto each bottom bun, then top with lettuce, a tomato slice, a cooked burger patty, and the top burger bun.

# Chapter 5

# Dinners

Tell your family you've got it covered tonight.

# Spaghetti Lo Mein

**Serves 4 • Total Time: 40 minutes**

BEGINNER ——————●———————— PRO

BEGINNER        PRO-IN-TRAINING        PRO

Traditionally, long fresh egg noodles are used in this Chinese American classic, but we opted for easy-to-find spaghetti, which is similar in texture.

| Ingredients | Amount |
| --- | --- |
| Kosher salt | |
| Spaghetti | ½ pound |
| Low-sodium chicken or vegetable broth | ½ cup |
| Hoisin sauce | 3 tablespoons |
| Low-sodium soy sauce | 2 tablespoons |
| Cornstarch | 1 teaspoon |
| Sesame oil | 2 teaspoons |
| Vegetable oil | 1 tablespoon |
| Broccoli | 1 medium head, cut into small florets |
| Red bell pepper | 1, cut into medium strips |
| Shredded carrots | 1 cup |
| Garlic | 2 cloves, minced |
| Ginger | 1 (2-inch) piece, peeled and minced |
| Green onions | 2, thinly sliced |
| Sesame seeds | 1 tablespoon |

> Chinese food and Chinese American food are like cousins: They share common ingredients and some similar cooking styles, but can taste and look very different.

**1. Boil noodles:** Fill a large pot with water and add a big pinch of salt. Bring to a boil over high heat. Cook pasta according to package instructions, then drain into a colander.

**2. Make sauce:** In a medium bowl, whisk together broth, hoisin sauce, soy sauce, cornstarch, and sesame oil.

**3. Cook veggies:** In a large skillet over medium heat, heat vegetable oil. Add broccoli and bell pepper and shake the panto distribute into a single layer. Cook undisturbed for 6 minutes, then stir with a wooden spoon, and keep stirring occasionally for 2 to 3 minutes longer, until vegetables are tender. Add carrot and cook 2 minutes, then add garlic and ginger and cook until fragrant, 1 to 2 minutes.

**4.** Add noodles to pan and toss with tongs to combine. Add prepared sauce and simmer, stirring frequently, until sauce thickens and coats the noodles, 2 to 3 minutes. Transfer to serving dish, top with green onions and sesame seeds, and serve hot.

# Perfect Pizza

**Makes 2 • Total Time: 2 hours 20 minutes**

BEGINNER    PRO-IN-TRAINING    PRO

You could use store–bought pizza dough, but making your own is so much more satisfying—and fun! This recipe is easy to work with and perfect for all your favorite toppings.

| Ingredients | Amount |
| --- | --- |
| **For the dough** | |
| **Cooking spray** | **For greasing** |
| **Lukewarm water** | **1¼ cups** |
| **Granulated sugar** | **1 tablespoon** |
| **Active dry yeast** | **1 (¼–ounce packet** |
| **All-purpose flour** | **3 cups, plus more for kneading** |
| **Extra-virgin olive oil** | **¼ cup** |
| **Kosher salt** | **2 teaspoons** |
| **For the pizza** | |
| **Extra-virgin olive oil** | **As needed** |
| **Coarse cornmeal** | **¼ cup** |
| **Marinara** | **1 cup** |
| **Fresh mozzarella** | **½ pound, thinly sliced** |
| **Fresh basil leaves** | **For topping** |

**What You'll Need**

2 Large Bowls

Small Bowl

Wooden Spoon

Clean Dish Towel

Large Baking Sheet

Rolling Pin

Basting Brush

Spoon

Oven Mitts

An off oven or empty microwave is a nice warm spot to proof your dough.

**1. Make dough:** Grease a large bowl with cooking spray and set aside. In a small bowl, stir together lukewarm water and sugar, then sprinkle yeast over water and let sit until frothy, about 8 minutes.

**2.** In another large bowl, add flour, oil, and salt. Pour in yeast mixture, then mix with a wooden spoon until a shaggy dough begins to form.

**3. Knead it:** Use your hands to knead against sides of bowl until dough starts to come together. Sprinkle about ½ cup flour onto a clean counter, then dump dough onto counter. Sprinkle top of dough with more flour. Knead dough until it feels elastic and only slightly sticky, about 5 minutes.

**4. Let rise:** Form dough into a tight ball, place in your oiled bowl, and cover with a clean dish towel. Let rise in a warm spot in your kitchen until doubled in size, about 1 hour 30 minutes.

**5.** Gently punch down dough, then divide in half. Roll each half on your counter to form a tight ball. (At this point, you can freeze one or make two pizzas.) Cover dough with towel and let rest as you preheat oven to 500°F, for at least 20 minutes.

**6. Roll it out:** Grease a large baking sheet with olive oil and sprinkle all over with half of the cornmeal. On a lightly floured surface, gently flatten one ball of dough and roll with a rolling pin (or stretch with your hands) until about 12 inches in diameter.

**7.** Carefully transfer to baking sheet and use your hands to reshape and stretch as needed. Use basting brush to lightly coat dough all over with oil. Then add ½ cup sauce to middle of dough and spread outward with a spoon, leaving a 1-inch border for the crust. Top with half of the fresh mozzarella.

**8. Bake it:** Bake until crust is golden and cheese is melty, 12 to 15 minutes. Top with fresh basil leaves and a drizzle of olive oil. Repeat with remaining dough and toppings.

# The Super-Fun History of PIZZA

that's amore!

PIZZERIA DI PIETRO E BASTA COSÌ

What do you love most about pizza: the sweet tomato sauce? The melty cheese? The spicy pepperoni? Whichever you pick, you can rest assured that none of them were used to make what the Italians called "pizza" back in the 11th century. **Their version was just plain baked dough, inspired by focaccia and Greek flatbreads, and it was a go-to meal for Italy's lower class.**

When King Umberto I and Queen Margherita visited Naples in 1889, they requested a taste of the city's best local food. The royal chef tapped pizzeria owner Raffaele Esposito to make pizza for the pair. **The queen's favorite pie was the one topped with foods representing the colors of the Italian flag: white mozzarella, green basil, and red tomatoes. It earned the name "pizza Margherita" in her honor.**

United States

Italy

Italians emigrated to the United States, and they brought their little slices of home with them. They opened pizza joints all along the East Coast, including some of the earliest pizzerias on record, at the beginning of the 20th century in New York. **Historians argue over what the very first spot was, but many claim it to be Lombardi's, which still exists in Manhattan's Little Italy neighborhood.**

Pizza continued to make its way all over the country—that's why there are so many regional styles. In Chicago, chefs churn out deep-dish pizzas that stand 1 to 2 inches high. Detroit is famous for baking thick, rectangular pizza that comes out a little bit chewy and a little bit crispy. And Californians have earned a reputation for topping thin crusts with fresh, local veggies. (Did you know that Hawaiians didn't invent the ham-and-pineapple combo called Hawaiian pizza? Canadians did!)

**Today there are more than 77,000 pizzerias in the U.S. alone—and the pizza market is a $45.73 billion industry.**

Chicago style

Detroit style

Hawaiian pizza

## Cooking With Grandma

Josephine's sauce will be your go-to for pasta!

**Josephine Rege** grew up in New Jersey during the Great Depression and learned to cook from her mom. **"She had a grocery store, and in the back, she would make spaghetti and [this] sauce. It would smell so good, people would come in and ask if she would sell it."** Her mom never wrote down how to make the sauce. Josephine watched, remembered, then years later recorded everything in a "little book."

Fast-forward to today, and Josephine's children and grand-children are making this very same tomato sauce. And thanks to Josephine, they know not to hover over the pan while the sauce simmers. **"Give it so many minutes and then stir,"** she says.

## What You'll Need

Large Skillet

Wooden Spoon

Fork

# Super-Simple Pasta Sauce

**Serves 4 • Total Time: 2 hours 20 minutes**

BEGINNER     PRO-IN-TRAINING     PRO

There's no shame in jarred marinara. But being able to make your own (really, really) good pasta sauce is a life skill that everyone should have. Serve it over spaghetti and use leftovers for English Muffin Pizzas (page 32).

| Ingredients | Amount |
| --- | --- |
| Extra-virgin olive oil | ¼ cup |
| Garlic | 1 clove |
| Whole peeled tomatoes | 1 (28-ounce) can |
| Water | 1½ cups |
| Tomato paste | 1 (6-ounce) can |
| Kosher salt | 1 tablespoon |
| Granulated sugar | 1 teaspoon |
| Parsley | ¼ cup, chopped |
| Dried basil | ¼ teaspoon |
| Freshly ground black pepper | ¼ teaspoon |
| Cooked pasta | For serving |

**1.** In a large skillet over medium heat, heat oil. Add garlic and cook, stirring occasionally with a wooden spoon, until golden, 5 minutes.

**2.** Add remaining ingredients. Use a fork to carefully smash tomatoes into bite-size pieces. Bring to a boil, then lower to a simmer, and cook for 2 hours, stirring occasionally.

**3.** Check for seasoning, adding more salt and pepper if necessary. Serve with pasta.

# Chili Cheese Dog Casserole

**Serves 8 • Total Time: 40 minutes**

BEGINNER          PRO-IN-TRAINING          PRO

Crescent rolls make everything better—especially hot dogs.

| Ingredients | Amount |
| --- | --- |
| Refrigerated crescent dough | 1 (8-ounce) tube |
| Shredded cheddar | 1 cup |
| Hot dogs | 8 |
| Chili | 2 (15-ounce) cans |
| Butter | 2 tablespoons, melted |
| Finely chopped chives | 1 teaspoon, plus more for topping |
| Garlic powder | ½ teaspoon |

Get crescent dough sheets if you can!

1. Preheat oven to 375°F. Roll out crescent dough and pinch the perforations together to seal. Cut into 8 even squares. Sprinkle cheddar on each square, then top with hot dog. Wrap dough around hot dog and pinch to seal.

2. Using a spoon, spread chili in an even layer on the bottom of a 9x13-inch baking dish. Place hot dogs side by side in a row on top of chili.

3. In a small bowl, combine melted butter with chives and garlic powder. Brush over hot dogs and bake for 30 minutes, covering with foil if crescent dough begins to get too dark.

4. Top with more chives and serve.

**What You'll Need**

Chef's Knife

Baking Dish

Spoon

Small Bowl

Basting Brush

Foil

Oven Mitts

# Flamin' Mac & Cheetos

**Serves 4 • Total Time: 30 minutes**

BEGINNER　　　PRO-IN-TRAINING　　　PRO

You'll find it hard not to fall head over heels in love with this spicy, crunchy, and somewhat crazy topping.

| Ingredients | Amount |
| --- | --- |
| Kosher salt | 1½ teaspoons, plus more for pasta |
| Cavatappi | 1 pound |
| Butter | ½ cup (1 stick) plus 3 tablespoons, divided |
| All-purpose flour | ½ cup |
| Cayenne pepper | 1 teaspoon, optional |
| Freshly ground black pepper | ½ tablespoon |
| Whole milk | 4 cups |
| Shredded cheddar | 4 cups, divided |
| Shredded pepper jack | 2 cups |
| Panko bread crumbs | ½ cup |
| Flamin' Hot Cheetos | ½ cup, crushed |

Don't like spicy? Original Cheetos will also work!

**What You'll Need**

Large Pot

Colander

Large Saucepan

Whisk

Baking Dish

Wooden Spoon

Small Skillet

Oven Mitts

**1.** Preheat oven to 350°F. Fill a large pot with water and add a big pinch of salt. Bring to a boil over high heat. Cook pasta according to package instructions, then drain into a colander.

**2.** Meanwhile, melt ½ cup butter in a large saucepan over medium heat. Sprinkle in flour, whisking to create a roux. If you want your sauce spicy, add cayenne. Add salt and pepper, then slowly pour in milk, whisking as you go. Keep whisking as it simmers and thickens, 5 to 6 minutes. Add cheddar and pepper jack, stirring until melted and combined. Remove mixture from heat.

**3.** Add pasta to a 9x13-inch baking dish and pour cheese sauce on top, stirring gently with a wooden spoon to combine.

**4.** In a small skillet, melt remaining 3 tablespoons butter over medium heat. Add panko and Cheetos, stirring constantly for 3 to 4 minutes, or until lightly golden. Sprinkle on top of pasta in an even layer. Bake 12 to 15 minutes, or until hot and bubbling.

# 10 Ways to Top Your Hot Dog

BEGINNER     PRO-IN-TRAINING     PRO

It's time to think beyond the ketchup and mustard.

**Mexican Street Corn** Toss a small scoop of **corn** with a spoonful of **mayonnaise**, a squeeze of **lime** juice, a pinch of **chili powder**, and some fresh **cilantro** leaves. Scoop on top of hot dog.

**Tropical** Top hot dog with chopped **pineapple** (or mango) and chopped **red onion**, then squeeze juice from a **lime** wedge on top.

**BLT** Spread **mayonnaise** on hot dog bun. Top hot dog with shredded **lettuce**, chopped **tomatoes**, and chopped cooked **bacon**.

**Pizza** Spread a spoonful of **pizza sauce** on top of hot dog then sprinkle with a big pinch of **shredded mozzarella**. Top with as much **mini pepperoni** as you want and a pinch of **dried oregano**. Bake at 350°F until melty.

**Queso** Drizzle some warm jarred **queso** on hot dog and sprinkle with crushed **blue tortilla chips.**

**French Onion Dip** Top hot dog with jarred **French onion dip** and crushed **potato chips.**

**BBQ** Top hot dog with prepared **coleslaw** and **barbecue sauce.**

**Frito Pie** Top hot dog with a big spoonful of warmed canned **chili**, crushed **Fritos**, and **shredded cheddar.**

**Jalapeño Popper** Spread some **cream cheese** on hot dog bun. Top hot dog with shredded **cheddar**, **pickled jalapeños**, and chopped cooked **bacon.**

**Mac & Cheese** Top hot dog with **macaroni and cheese.** (Use leftovers from page 102!)

# Oven-Baked BBQ Chicken

**Serves 8 · Total Time: 2 hours 5 minutes**

BEGINNER ——●—— PRO-IN-TRAINING —— PRO

Barbecue chicken doesn't have to be a summer exclusive.
Our oven-baked version is a winner year-round!

## What You'll Need

Large Bowl

Plastic Wrap

Large Baking Sheet

Aluminum Foil

Basting Brush

Oven Mitts

| Ingredients | Amount |
| --- | --- |
| **For the barbecue sauce** | |
| Ketchup | 1½ cups |
| Brown sugar | 1 cup, packed |
| Water | ½ cup |
| Apple cider vinegar | ¼ cup |
| Worcestershire sauce | 1 tablespoon |
| Molasses | 1 tablespoon |
| Kosher salt | 1½ teaspoons |
| Garlic powder | ½ teaspoon |
| Onion powder | ½ teaspoon |
| Ground mustard | ¼ teaspoon |
| **For the chicken** | |
| Bone-in skin-on chicken | 3 pounds → Thighs, drumsticks, and breasts! |
| Large onions | 2, thinly sliced |
| Extra-virgin olive oil | 1 tablespoon |

**1. Make barbecue sauce:** In a large bowl, combine ketchup, brown sugar, water, apple cider vinegar, Worcestershire, molasses, salt, and spices. Reserve 1 cup of sauce for later. Add chicken to remaining barbecue sauce. Cover with plastic wrap and refrigerate for at least 1 hour and up to overnight.

**2. Make chicken:** Preheat oven to 425°F and line a large baking sheet with aluminum foil. Place onions on baking sheet, drizzle with oil, and toss to coat. Place chicken on top of onions, skin side up, and bake until golden and internal temperature reaches 165°F, 30 to 40 minutes. Remove baking sheet from oven.

**3.** Grab an adult for help, and switch oven to broil. Brush chicken with reserved barbecue sauce on both sides and broil until skin is crispy and sauce is thickened, 5 minutes.

## Cooking With Grandma

Kongmay's recipe is a family favorite!

**Kongmay Bouavichith** raised her children in **Savannakhet, a small Laotian city on the banks of the Mekong River.** After the Vietnam War, she and her family were refugees in Thailand before moving to rural southwestern Minnesota.

Kongmay planted a large garden at her new home, where she harvested fresh produce for dinner. **She taught her children to cook with color—because good-looking food tastes better—** and to always adjust a recipe to fit their tastes.

# Laap

**Serves 4 · Total Time: 25 minutes**

BEGINNER      PRO-IN-TRAINING      PRO

Laos is a landlocked country in Southeast Asia, and much of the food is built on sour and spicy flavors. If you're not into super-spicy food, add just a little bit of chile paste.

| Ingredients | Amount |
| --- | --- |
| Limes | 3, divided |
| Ground chicken or pork | 1 pound |
| Vegetable oil | 1 tablespoon |
| Palm sugar or granulated sugar | 1 teaspoon |
| Fish sauce | 1 tablespoon |
| Shallots | 2, finely chopped |
| Fresh mint | 1 handful, roughly chopped |
| Fresh cilantro | 1 handful, roughly chopped |
| Green onions | 2, roughly chopped |
| Chile paste | 1 tablespoon, or to taste |
| Toasted jasmine rice powder | 2 tablespoons, divided, optional |
| Sticky rice | For serving, optional |
| Lettuce leaves | For serving, optional |
| Cucumber slices | For serving, optional |

**1.** In a large bowl, combine juice of 1 lime with ground meat.

**2.** In medium skillet over medium-high heat, heat oil. Add marinated ground meat and cook, breaking up meat with a wooden spoon, until meat is cooked through and golden, 6 minutes. Stir sugar into meat, then remove pan from heat.

**3.** In a second large bowl, combine fish sauce and juice from 2 remaining limes. Add ground meat mixture to the bowl and stir well. Add shallots, herbs, and green onions and continue mixing (as the meat cools, its heat will begin to release the flavor of the herbs and onions). Add chile paste to taste, and all but 1 teaspoon rice powder if using, and stir well to combine.

**4.** Garnish with remaining rice powder if using, then serve with sticky rice ("khao niao"), wrapped in lettuce leaves, on slices of cucumber, or eat on its own!

# Cheesy Tomato Squiggles

Serves 6 • Total Time: 30 minutes

BEGINNER          PRO-IN-TRAINING          PRO

This super-curly special type of fusilli is the most
fun pasta of all time. Plus, the sauce clings to it better!

| Ingredients | Amount |
| --- | --- |
| Fusilli corti bucati | 1 pound |
| Extra-virgin olive oil | 1 tablespoon |
| Garlic | 3 cloves, minced |
| Tomato paste | 1 (6-ounce) can |
| Heavy cream | 1 cup |
| Freshly grated Parmesan | ½ cup, plus more for serving |
| Kosher salt | |
| Freshly ground black pepper | |
| Butter | 4 tablespoons |

### What You'll Need

- Large Pot
- Liquid Measuring Cup
- Colander
- Large High-Sided Skillet
- Wooden Spoon
- Whisk

1. Fill a large pot with water and add a big pinch of salt. Bring to a boil over high heat. Cook pasta according to package instructions. Ask an adult to help scoop out about ¾ cup pasta water with a liquid measuring cup, then drain pasta into a colander.

2. In a large high-sided skillet over medium heat, heat oil. Add garlic and cook, stirring occasionally with a wooden spoon, until fragrant and just starting to turn golden, 1 to 2 minutes. Add tomato paste and cook until darkened, 3 minutes more.

3. Slowly add cream and whisk until mixture is smooth. Add ½ cup Parmesan and stir until melted. Season with salt and pepper.

4. Add pasta, butter, and ½ cup reserved pasta water to skillet and toss to coat. Add more pasta water, 1 tablespoon at a time, to make sauce thinner if needed.

5. Sprinkle with more Parmesan before serving.

# Best-Ever Fettuccine Alfredo

**Serves 4 • Total Time: 20 minutes**

BEGINNER    PRO-IN-TRAINING    PRO

This recipe is so good, you'll want to memorize it. Luckily, it's a super-simple one to remember.

| Ingredients | Amount |
| --- | --- |
| Fettuccine | 1 pound |
| Heavy cream | ½ cup |
| Butter | ½ cup (1 stick) |
| Freshly grated Parmesan | ½ cup |
| Kosher salt | |
| Freshly ground black pepper | |
| Freshly chopped parsley | 2 tablespoons |

1. Fill a large pot with water and a big pinch of salt. Bring to a boil over high heat. Cook pasta according to package instructions. Ask an adult to help scoop out about 1 cup pasta water with a liquid measuring cup, then drain pasta into a colander.

2. In a large high-sided skillet over medium heat, add cream and butter. Cook until butter is melted and cream is heated through. Whisk in Parmesan, then add a pinch of salt and a few grinds of pepper. Taste the sauce and add more salt and pepper if necessary.

3. Add cooked pasta to skillet and toss with tongs until pasta is coated in sauce. If sauce is too thick, add reserved pasta water, 1 tablespoon at a time, until it's creamy. Top with parsley and serve immediately.

**What You'll Need**

Large Pot

Liquid Measuring Cup

Colander

Large High-Sided Skillet

Whisk

Tongs

If your sauce "breaks," which means it separates and becomes grainy, toss the pasta with some more reserved pasta water to get it nice and creamy again.

# Baked Pineapple Salmon

**Serves 4 • Total Time: 55 minutes**

BEGINNER          PRO-IN-TRAINING          PRO

This dish is the perfect mix of sweet and savory. Serve it straight off the baking sheet, with lime wedges on the side.

| Ingredients | Amount |
| --- | --- |
| Cooking spray | For pan |
| Pineapple rings | 12, fresh or canned |
| Salmon fillets | 4 (3-ounce) pieces, patted dry with paper towels |
| Kosher salt | |
| Freshly ground black pepper | |
| Butter | 3 tablespoons, melted |
| Sweet chili sauce | 3 tablespoons |
| Cilantro | 2 tablespoons, freshly chopped |
| Garlic | 3 cloves, minced |
| Ginger | 2 teaspoons, freshly grated |
| Toasted sesame oil | 2 teaspoons |
| Crushed red pepper flakes | ½ teaspoon, optional |
| Toasted sesame seeds | For topping |
| Green onions | For topping, thinly sliced |
| Lime wedges | For serving |

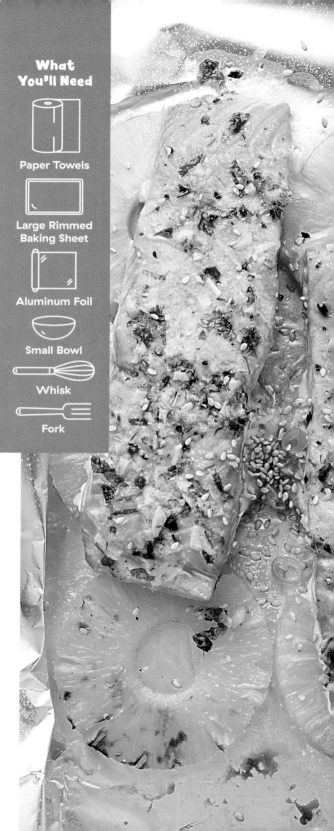

**What You'll Need**

Paper Towels

Large Rimmed Baking Sheet

Aluminum Foil

Small Bowl

Whisk

Fork

1. Preheat oven to 350°F. Line a large rimmed baking sheet with aluminum foil and grease with cooking spray. Create 4 rows of pineapple, with 3 slices in each row.

2. Season both sides of salmon fillets with salt and pepper. Place one piece of salmon on top of each row of pineapple.

3. In a small bowl, whisk together butter, chili sauce, cilantro, garlic, ginger, sesame oil, and red pepper flakes, if using. Pour a little bit of sauce over each piece of salmon.

4. Bake until salmon is opaque and easily flakes with a fork, about 20 minutes.

5. Grab an adult for help, and switch oven to broil. Broil for 2 minutes, or until fish looks sticky and slightly charred in spots.

6. Top with sesame seeds and green onions and serve with lime wedges.

## Cooking With Grandma

**Make Janis's shrimp dinner tonight!**

**Janis Curry** grew up in Louisiana, where she first learned to cook from her mom. But it was in Philadelphia that she got some of her **most important cooking lessons** from her cousins. They taught her the importance of cleaning as you go, making certain you have everything you need before getting started on a recipe, and not cooking anything over high heat.

The biggest lesson she wants to share with her grandsons is to appreciate the cook, not just the food. **"The cook is usually cooking with love and that's important to remember."** For this recipe, she encourages you to switch it up according to your own personal taste. Sausage and chicken are great substitutes for shrimp!

# Okra & Shrimp

**Serves 4 • Total Time: 50 minutes**

BEGINNER — PRO-IN-TRAINING — PRO

Although it's technically a fruit (it's filled with seeds!), okra is eaten like a vegetable in savory dishes. It is popular in the South but often gets a bad rep for being slimy. Don't worry—the acidity from the tomatoes helps combat that texture here.

| Ingredients | Amount |
| --- | --- |
| Extra-virgin olive oil | 1 tablespoon |
| Onion | 1, diced |
| Garlic | 2 cloves, minced |
| Frozen cut okra | 1 (16-ounce) bag |
| Frozen corn | 1 (10-ounce) bag |
| Diced fire-roasted tomatoes | 1 (28-ounce) can |
| Dried oregano | 2 teaspoons |
| Dried thyme | 2 teaspoons |
| Smoked paprika | 1 tablespoon |
| Bay leaf | 1 |
| Kosher salt | |
| Freshly ground black pepper | |
| Jumbo shrimp | 1 pound, peeled and deveined |
| Parsley | Freshly chopped, for topping |

**1.** In a large, deep skillet on medium-high heat, heat oil. Add onion and garlic, stir with a wooden spoon, and cook until onion is soft, 5 minutes.

**2.** Add okra, corn, tomatoes, oregano, thyme, paprika, and bay leaf. Reduce heat to low and bring ingredients to a simmer. If mixture is looking too thick, add 1 tablespoon water. Season with salt and pepper, cover with a lid, and simmer over low heat, 10 minutes.

**3.** Stir in shrimp, then cover and cook until shrimp are pink and opaque, 6 to 8 minutes. Season to taste with salt and pepper, then top with parsley before serving.

# Philly Cheesesteak Lettuce Wraps

Serves 4 • Total Time: 30 minutes

BEGINNER — PRO-IN-TRAINING — PRO

You'll never get tired of the classic combination of seared steak, sautéed peppers and onions, and melty provolone cheese. And no, we didn't forget the buns! Lettuce makes the perfect wrap.

| Ingredients | Amount |
| --- | --- |
| Vegetable oil | 2 tablespoons, divided |
| Large onion | 1, thinly sliced |
| Large bell peppers | 2, thinly sliced |
| Dried oregano | 1 teaspoon |
| Kosher salt | |
| Freshly ground black pepper | |
| Skirt steak | 1 pound, thinly sliced |
| Shredded provolone | 1 cup |
| Large butterhead lettuce leaves | 8 |
| Freshly chopped parsley | 1 tablespoon |

1. In a large skillet over medium heat, heat 1 tablespoon oil. Add onion and bell peppers and season with oregano, salt, and pepper. Cook, stirring often, until vegetables are tender, about 5 minutes. Remove peppers and onions from skillet and heat remaining 1 tablespoon oil in skillet.

2. Add steak in a single layer and season with salt and pepper. Cook until steak is seared on one side, about 2 minutes. Flip and cook until steak is seared on the second side and cooked to your liking, 2 minutes more for medium (about 140°F).

3. Return onion mixture to skillet and toss to combine. Sprinkle provolone over steak and onions, then cover skillet with a tight-fitting lid and cook until cheese has melted, 1 minute. Remove from heat.

4. Arrange lettuce on a serving platter. Scoop steak mixture onto each piece of lettuce. Top with parsley and serve warm.

# Chapter 6

# SWEETS

There's always room
for dessert.

# Edible Cookie Dough

**Serves 10 • Total Time: 10 minutes**

BEGINNER    PRO-IN-TRAINING    PRO

Attention, all cookie dough lovers! This recipe is meant to be eaten by the spoonful (no raw eggs or flour in here!). Can you tell what the secret ingredient is?

Any type of milk works!

| Ingredients | Amount |
| --- | --- |
| Butter | ¾ cup (1½ sticks), softened |
| Brown sugar | ¾ cup, packed |
| Pure vanilla extract | 1½ teaspoons |
| Graham cracker crumbs | 1⅔ cups (11 graham cracker sheets) |
| Milk | 2½ tablespoons |
| Kosher salt | ½ teaspoon |
| Mini chocolate chips | ⅔ cup |

**1.** In a large bowl using a hand mixer or in the bowl of a stand mixer, beat butter, brown sugar, and vanilla until light and fluffy.

**2.** Add graham cracker crumbs, milk, and salt and mix until fully incorporated.

**3.** Using a spatula, fold in chocolate chips and serve immediately.

**What You'll Need**

Large Bowl

Mixer

Spatula

**Warning!**
Don't try baking the dough! We did and the results were disastrous. Without an egg, flour, or a leavener such as baking powder or baking soda, the sugar burns and the butter seeps out.

For double–chocolate cookie dough (hello!), sub in ¼ cup of cocoa powder for ¼ cup of the graham cracker crumbs.

# Mini Boston Cream Pies

**Makes 40 • Total Time: 25 minutes**

BEGINNER          PRO-IN-TRAINING          PRO

Did you know Boston cream pie isn't pie at all? It's actually a cake composed of two layers of sponge cake, filled with vanilla custard, and topped with chocolate glaze. No baking is needed for our mini icebox cake version, which uses one of our all-time favorite sweet snacks: Nilla Wafers.

| Ingredients | Amount |
| --- | --- |
| Instant vanilla pudding | 1 (3.4-ounce) package |
| Whole milk | 1 cup, cold |
| Whipped topping | 1½ cups |
| Semisweet chocolate chips | ¾ cup |
| Heavy cream | ⅓ cup |
| Nilla Wafers | 1 (11-ounce) box |

## What You'll Need

- Large Bowl
- Whisk
- Spatula
- Piping Bag
- Medium Bowl
- Small Saucepan
- Serving Dish
- Spoon

## 1. Make filling:
In a large bowl, whisk together vanilla pudding mix and milk until thick. Fold in whipped topping and transfer mixture to a piping bag. Refrigerate until ready to use.

## 2. Make ganache:
Add chocolate chips to a medium bowl. In a small saucepan over medium heat, heat heavy cream until bubbles form around the edges. Pour heavy cream over chocolate chips and let sit 2 minutes, then whisk until smooth. Let cool slightly.

## 3. Assemble pies:
Cut the end of the piping bag and pipe filling onto the flat side of a Nilla Wafer. Top with another Nilla Wafer to create a sandwich; transfer to a serving dish. Repeat with remaining filling.

## 4. Top it off:
Spoon ganache on top of each cream pie before serving.

**Craving cookies?
Bake Marcia's
amazing recipe!**

Marcia Saltz grew up in a two-family house in Bergen, New Jersey, with her parents, aunt, uncle, three cousins, and three grandparents. Everyone in the family raved about her maternal grandmother's cooking, but her grandmother didn't want to share her recipes. So most of what Marcia learned in the kitchen came from watching her mother cook.

Marcia's good friend Rita shared this recipe with her and another friend, Roberta. And since then, it has turned into a big family affair. "I hope that my grandchildren learn that sharing food is more than just eating. Making an ancestor's recipe is comforting and makes one feel as though the person is still with them."

Large Bowl

Mixer

Plastic Wrap

2 Baking Sheets

Parchment Paper

Small Bowl

Fork

Rolling Pin

Round Cookie Cutter

Basting Brush

Oven Mitts

# Hamantaschen

**Makes 24 • Total Time: 3 hours 30 minutes**

BEGINNER ——●—— PRO-IN-TRAINING —— PRO

Hamantaschen, pronounced *HA–men–ta–shen,* are shortbread–like cookies filled with jam traditionally served around the Jewish holiday of Purim.

| Ingredients | Amount |
| --- | --- |
| Butter | 1 cup (2 sticks), softened |
| Granulated sugar | 1 cup |
| Large eggs | 4, divided |
| All-purpose flour | 3½ cups, plus more for surface |
| Baking powder | 1½ teaspoons |
| Kosher salt | 1 teaspoon |
| Pure vanilla extract | 1 teaspoon |
| Solo raspberry fruit filling | 1 (12-ounce) can |

**1.** In a large bowl using a hand mixer or in the bowl of a stand mixer, beat butter and sugar until light and fluffy. Add 3 eggs and beat until fully incorporated, then add flour, baking powder, salt, and vanilla, and mix until just combined. Cover bowl with plastic wrap and refrigerate overnight.

**2.** Preheat oven to 375°F and line two large baking sheets with parchment paper. In a small bowl, beat remaining egg to use as egg wash.

**3.** On a well-floured surface, roll out half the dough until about ¼-inch thick, keeping remaining half of dough cold. Use a round cookie cutter (or clean Solo can!) dipped in flour to cut out circles.

**4.** Brush each circle with egg wash then top with a heaping teaspoon of filling. To form each cookie, bring up three corners of circle then pinch and twist to form a triangle. Place on prepared baking sheet and brush with more egg wash.

**5.** Bake until cookies are golden on bottoms, 12 to 15 minutes.

**6.** Repeat with remaining dough and filling.

# Cookie Bars

**Makes 16 · Total Time: 45 minutes**

BEGINNER     PRO-IN-TRAINING     PRO

Chocolate chips are great, but let's be real—
you can do better. Follow our basic cookie bar
recipe, then go all out with the mix-ins.

| Ingredients | Amount |
| --- | --- |
| Cooking spray | As needed |
| Butter | ¾ cup (1½ sticks), softened |
| Granulated sugar | ¾ cup |
| Brown sugar | ½ cup, packed |
| Large eggs | 2 |
| Pure vanilla extract | 1 teaspoon |
| All-purpose flour | 2 cups |
| Baking powder | ¾ teaspoon |
| Kosher salt | ½ teaspoon |
| Crunchy mix-ins | 1½ cups |
| Peanut butter, Nutella, or marshmallow creme | ½ cup, warmed for 15 seconds in microwave |

**1.** Preheat oven to 350°F and grease a 9x13-inch pan with
cooking spray. In a large bowl using a hand mixer or in the
bowl of a stand mixer, beat butter and both sugars until light
and creamy. Add eggs and vanilla and beat until combined.

**2.** In a medium bowl, whisk together flour, baking powder,
and salt. Add dry ingredients to wet ingredients and beat
until just combined. Fold in 1½ cups total of crunchy mix-ins.

**3.** Transfer dough to prepared pan and smooth top with
spatula. Dollop peanut butter, Nutella, or marshmallow creme
on top and use a butter knife to swirl into dough.

**4.** Bake until golden and a toothpick inserted into the middle
comes out with a few crumbs, 30 to 35 minutes. Let cool
before slicing into squares.

## What You'll Need

Baking Pan

Large Bowl

Mixer

Medium Bowl

Whisk

Spatula

Butter Knife

Toothpick

Chef's Knife

Oven Mitts

## Crunchy Mix-Ins

Here are 11 solid
options, but
you probably
have some ideas
of your own.
(Choose up to 3!)

**Crushed graham crackers**

**Mini marshmallows**

**Chopped soft caramels**

**Rainbow sprinkles**

**Peanut butter chips**

**Crushed potato chips**

**Chocolate chips**

**Chopped candy bars**

**Bake the cover!**
Add white chocolate chips and rainbow sprinkles to dough, then drizzle baked bars with melted white chocolate.

**Crushed pretzels**

**Shredded coconut**

**Salty popcorn**

129

# Mason Jar Ice Cream

**Serves 2 • Total Time: 3 hours 10 minutes**

BEGINNER      PRO-IN-TRAINING      PRO

All you need is a Mason jar (and some major muscle) to whip up this legit vanilla ice cream.

| Ingredients | Amount |
| --- | --- |
| Heavy cream | 1 cup |
| Granulated sugar | 1½ tablespoons |
| Pure vanilla extract | ½ teaspoon |
| Kosher salt | Pinch |

1. Pour cream, sugar, vanilla, and salt into a large Mason jar and secure tightly with a lid. Shake the jar until cream thickens and almost doubles in size, 4 to 5 minutes. It should be opaque and easily coat the back of a wooden spoon.

2. Freeze for 3 hours, or until hardened. Use an ice-cream scoop to serve with your favorite toppings.

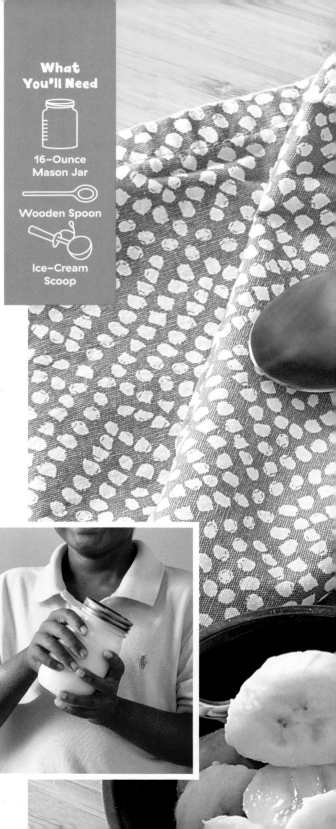

What You'll Need

16-Ounce Mason Jar

Wooden Spoon

Ice-Cream Scoop

# Mix It Up!

If vanilla isn't your vibe, try adding these sweet combos to your jar before shaking.

## Peanut Butter Explosion

 1 tablespoon **smooth peanut butter**

+

 2 **Reese's Cups**, roughly chopped

## Banana Split

 1 chopped **banana**

+

 1 tablespoon **rainbow sprinkles**

+

 4 **maraschino cherries**, quartered

## Sweet 'n' Salty

 6 **pretzels**, crushed

+

 2 tablespoons **mini M&M's**

+

 2 tablespoons chopped **honey-roasted peanuts**

# Perfect Fudgy Brownies

**Makes 24 • Total Time: 55 minutes**

BEGINNER          PRO-IN-TRAINING          PRO

Brace yourself for the FUDGIEST. BROWNIES. EVER. It took us 13 tests, 28 cups of chocolate chips, 3 dozen eggs, and 3 pounds of butter to get here, but we made it.

| Ingredients | Amount |
| --- | --- |
| Cooking spray | For pan |
| All-purpose flour | ¾ cup |
| Kosher salt | 1 teaspoon |
| Semisweet chocolate chips | 4 cups, divided |
| Butter | 1 cup (2 sticks), cut into large chunks |
| Granulated sugar | 1⅓ cups |
| Large eggs | 4 |
| Egg yolks | 2 |

**1.** Preheat oven to 350°F. Line a 9x13-inch baking pan with parchment paper and grease with cooking spray. In a small bowl, whisk together flour and salt.

**2.** Fill a saucepan with 2 inches of water and bring to a simmer over medium heat. Set a large heatproof bowl on top of saucepan to create a double boiler. Add 3 cups chocolate chips and butter to bowl and stir occasionally until melted. Carefully remove bowl from heat, then whisk in sugar.

**3.** Add eggs one at a time, whisking for 1 whole minute after each egg, then add egg yolks and whisk for 1 minute more.

**4.** Fold in flour mixture with a spatula until combined, then fold in remaining 1 cup chocolate chips.

**5.** Pour batter into prepared pan and smooth top with spatula. Bake until a toothpick inserted in middle comes out with a few moist crumbs, 28 to 30 minutes. Let cool in pan for 30 minutes before using parchment paper to remove brownies.

**What You'll Need**

Baking Pan

Parchment Paper

Small Bowl

Saucepan

Large Heatproof Bowl

Whisk

Spatula

Oven Mitts

Toothpick

**FYI!**
This step gives you a magical, crackly top!

Egg yolks make these brownies extra fudgy and decadent.

# Milk 'n' Cookies Icebox Cake

**Serves 8 to 10 · Total Time: 6 hours 20 minutes**

BEGINNER    PRO-IN-TRAINING    PRO

You need only four ingredients—and a little bit of patience—to make an out-of-this-world delicious icebox cake.

| Ingredients | Amount |
| --- | --- |
| Crunchy chocolate chip cookies | 2 (13-ounce) packages, divided |
| Heavy cream | 3 cups, cold |
| Cream cheese | 1 (8-ounce) block, cold |
| Powdered sugar | 2 tablespoons |

*The world's most perfect combination...*

*...in glorious cake form!*

## What You'll Need

Large Resealable Plastic Bag

Rolling Pin

Large Liquid Measuring Cup

Strainer

Mixer

Spatula

2 Large Bowls

Cake Plate

Plastic Wrap

**1.** In a large resealable bag, crush 15 chocolate chip cookies with a rolling pin. Transfer most of the crushed cookies to a large liquid measuring cup (save some for decorating at the end!) and add heavy cream. Let sit 10 minutes.

**2.** Pour heavy cream over strainer into a large bowl; discard crushed cookies.

**3.** Add cream cheese to another large bowl, then, using a handheld electric mixer, beat cream cheese until fluffy, 1 minute. Add sugar and beat until smooth, then add cookie–infused cream and beat until soft peaks form.

**4.** Spread a thin layer of whipped cream mixture on a cake plate. Arrange 8 cookies side by side in a circle, placing 3 cookies in the center. Spread a layer of whipped cream on top, and top with another layer of cookies (alternating so the cookies aren't placed directly on top). Repeat until you have six layers, ending with whipped cream.

**5.** Top with crushed cookies, then wrap loosely with plastic wrap and transfer to the fridge until very soft, 6 hours.

# Homemade Vanilla Cupcakes

**Makes 16 • Total Time: 50 minutes**

BEGINNER　　　PRO-IN-TRAINING　　　PRO

This is one of those recipes everyone will love—get ready to become the official birthday baker in your family.

| Ingredients | Amount |
| --- | --- |
| **For the cupcakes** | |
| Butter | 1 cup (2 sticks), softened |
| Granulated sugar | 1½ cups |
| Large eggs | 3 |
| Pure vanilla extract | 1 tablespoon |
| All-purpose flour | 2 cups |
| Cornstarch | 3 tablespoons |
| Baking powder | 1½ teaspoons |
| Kosher salt | 1 teaspoon |
| Whole milk | ¾ cup |
| **For the frosting** | |
| Butter | 1 cup (2 sticks), softened |
| Powdered sugar | 4 cups |
| Pure vanilla extract | 1 teaspoon |
| Heavy cream | ¼ cup |
| Kosher salt | Pinch |
| Rainbow sprinkles | For topping |

## What You'll Need

- 2 Muffin Tins
- Muffin Liners
- 3 Large Bowls
- Mixer
- Whisk
- Toothpick
- Spatula
- Piping Bag
- Piping Tip
- Oven Mitts

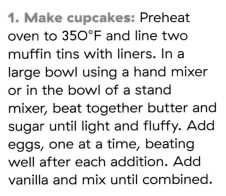

1. **Make cupcakes:** Preheat oven to 350°F and line two muffin tins with liners. In a large bowl using a hand mixer or in the bowl of a stand mixer, beat together butter and sugar until light and fluffy. Add eggs, one at a time, beating well after each addition. Add vanilla and mix until combined.

2. In another large bowl whisk together flour, cornstarch, baking powder, and salt. Add half the dry ingredients to the wet ingredients, beating until just combined. Pour in the milk and mix until fully incorporated. Add remaining dry ingredients and stir until just combined.

3. Fill cupcake liners three-quarters full with batter. Bake until slightly golden on top and a toothpick inserted into the middle comes out clean, about 25 minutes. Remove from pan and let cool completely.

4. **Meanwhile, make frosting:** In a large bowl using a hand mixer or in the bowl of a stand mixer, beat butter until fluffy. Add powdered sugar and beat until combined, then add vanilla, heavy cream, and salt and beat until combined.

5. Using a spatula, transfer to a piping bag fitted with a wide piping tip and decorate as desired. Top with sprinkles.

# Fried Ice Cream

**Serves 4 • Total Time: 45 minutes**

BEGINNER     PRO-IN-TRAINING     PRO

The next time you go to a fair, get some deep-fried ice cream. Until then, make this instead. (It's not really fried, but it tastes just as good!)

| Ingredients | Amount |
| --- | --- |
| Ice cream | 1 pint |
| Cornflakes | 1¼ cups, crushed |
| Butter | 1½ tablespoons |
| Ground cinnamon | ½ teaspoon |
| Granulated sugar | 2 teaspoons |
| Whipped cream | For topping |
| Sprinkles | For topping |
| Maraschino cherries | 4, for topping |

**What You'll Need**

Small Baking Sheet

Parchment Paper

Ice-Cream Scoop

Resealable Plastic Bag

Rolling Pin

Medium Skillet

Wooden Spoon

Shallow Bowl

**1.** Line a small baking sheet with parchment paper and place in freezer for 30 minutes. Once the baking sheet is chilled, scoop ice cream into 4 balls and place on sheet. Return to freezer while making cereal mixture, at least 30 minutes.

**2.** Meanwhile, put cereal in a large resealable plastic bag and let out as much air as possible before sealing. Use a rolling pin to crush cereal into very small pieces. It should almost have the texture of coarse sand.

**3.** In a medium skillet over medium heat, melt butter. Add cornflakes and cinnamon and cook, stirring occasionally, until cereal turns golden, 5 to 7 minutes. Carefully remove from heat and stir in sugar. Transfer to a shallow bowl to cool completely.

**4.** Remove ice-cream balls from freezer and roll in cooled cereal mixture to coat evenly. Top with whipped cream, sprinkles, and a cherry and serve immediately.

# Cooking With Grandma

**You'll love Shiro's sweet treat!**

**Shiromi Akka**, or Shiro, as her friends call her, grew up in Sri Lanka surrounded by fruit trees. Her grandfather was an avid gardener but it was her grandmother, along with her two great-aunts, who taught her how to cook.

When we asked her for a recipe, **coconut rock** was top of mind. This **"culinary delight,"** as Shiro likes to call it, is typically made with a fresh coconut, but she says using the frozen stuff is just as good. **When she was growing up, it was often served as a teatime pick-me-up treat before dinner.**

# Coconut Rock

**Makes 16 • Total Time: 1 hour 20 minutes**

BEGINNER     PRO-IN-TRAINING     PRO

This sweet Sri Lankan dessert is stunningly beautiful. Choosing the dye color is half the fun.

| Ingredients | Amount |
| --- | --- |
| Butter | For baking dish |
| Granulated sugar | ½ cup |
| Unflavored gelatin | 2 (0.25–ounce) packets |
| Water | ½ cup |
| Frozen grated coconut | 1 (16–ounce) package |
| Pure vanilla or almond extract | 2 teaspoons |
| Food coloring | 2 drops, any color! |

**1.** Lightly butter a 9x9–inch baking dish. In a small bowl, combine sugar and gelatin with a wooden spoon.

**2.** In a medium high–sided nonstick pan over medium heat, combine water and sugar mixture. Stir constantly with a wooden spoon, until sugar mixture has completely dissolved, 3 to 5 minutes.

**3.** Add coconut, extract, and a couple of drops of food coloring and stir thoroughly to combine. (You're going for a pastel shade, so start with only 2 drops of food coloring!)

**4.** Continue stirring until the mixture begins to crystallize on the sides of the pan. Ask an adult to very carefully transfer it to the baking dish and press into an even layer, about ½ inch thick.

**5.** Let cool for 1 hour before slicing into squares.

# Cinnamon Roll Rice Krispies Treats

**Makes 12 • Total Time: 1 hour**

BEGINNER     PRO-IN-TRAINING     PRO

One of our favorite parts of working in the Delish test kitchen is coming up with cool new mash-ups. And if there's one thing we know for sure, it's that you can turn almost anything into a "cinnamon roll." Pancakes, cheesecake, oatmeal, and, yes, Rice Krispies treats.

| Ingredients | Amount |
| --- | --- |
| **For the treats** | |
| Butter | ½ cup (1 stick), plus more for pan |
| Marshmallows | 1 (12-ounce) bag |
| Ground cinnamon | 1 teaspoon, plus more for dusting |
| Kosher salt | ¼ teaspoon |
| Rice Krispies | 5 cups |
| **For the glaze** | |
| Cream cheese | 1 ounce, softened |
| Powdered sugar | ¼ cup |
| Pure vanilla extract | ¼ teaspoon |
| Heavy cream | ½ teaspoon, plus more as needed |

**What You'll Need**

Baking Pan

Large Pot

Wooden Spoon

Spatula

Chef's Knife

Medium Bowl

Whisk

Piping Bag

Save those butter wrappers! You can use them to grease your pan.

**1. Make Rice Krispies treats:** Grease an 8x8–inch baking pan with butter. In a large pot over medium heat, melt remaining ½ cup butter. Add marshmallows and stir until completely melted. Stir in cinnamon and salt, then remove from heat and stir in Rice Krispies using a wooden spoon.

**2.** Pour mixture into pan and gently smooth top with spatula. Let cool for 25 minutes, then cut into 12 squares. Use your hands to round the edges and shape into round discs—like cinnamon rolls. (If the mixture is sticking to your hands, try wetting your palms with water before shaping.) Let cool completely.

**3. Meanwhile, make glaze:** In a medium bowl using a whisk, beat cream cheese until smooth. Add powdered sugar and vanilla and beat until smooth. If icing is too thick, add heavy cream ½ teaspoon at a time until it reaches desired consistency. Transfer to a piping bag (or resealable plastic bag).

**4.** Cut off tip of the piping bag and pipe swirls of frosting onto each Rice Krispies treat. Dust with cinnamon before serving.

# Take a Poke Cake Adventure!

**Serves 12 • Total Time: 1 hour**

BEGINNER     PRO-IN-TRAINING     PRO

When it comes to poke cakes, the possibilities are endless. We'll guide you through the process, but you get to choose all the flavors. The cake is your canvas and you are the artist.

**1**

**Pick your cake mix.** Preheat oven to 350°F, then line a 9x13-inch baking pan with parchment paper and grease with **cooking spray**. Prepare **cake mix** according to package instructions and let cool. After cake has cooled, use the handle of a wooden spoon to poke holes all over the cake.

Vanilla cake

Chocolate cake

**2**

**Pick your filling.** In a small microwave-safe bowl, microwave 1½ cups of your **favorite filling** until pourable, about 15 seconds. Then pour filling over the holes and smooth top of cake with a spatula.

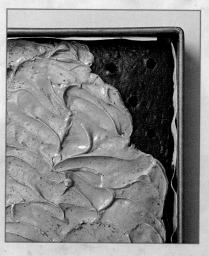

Caramel

Marshmallow creme

Nutella

Peanut butter

Hot fudge

**3**

**Frost it.** Use a spatula to spread **whipped topping** (it tastes good with everything!) on top of cake, making swoops to add texture to the top.

**4**

**Pick your decorations.** Sprinkle your decoration of choice on top of frosted cake.

*Crushed cookies*

*Sprinkles*

*Candies*

*Fresh fruit*

# Giant Strawberry Donut Cake

**Serves 10 · Total Time: 2 hours**

BEGINNER          PRO-IN-TRAINING          PRO

Like a strawberry glazed donut, but 12 times bigger (and better).

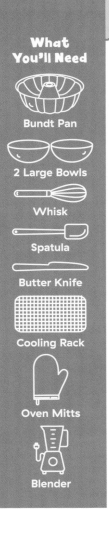

**What You'll Need**

Bundt Pan

2 Large Bowls

Whisk

Spatula

Butter Knife

Cooling Rack

Oven Mitts

Blender

| Ingredients | Amount |
| --- | --- |
| Cooking spray | For pan |
| White cake mix | 1 box |
| Sour cream | 1 cup |
| Whole milk | ¼ cup |
| Butter | ½ cup (1 stick), melted |
| Pure vanilla extract | 1 teaspoon |
| Large eggs | 2 |
| Strawberries, chopped | ½ cup |
| Cream cheese | 4 ounces, softened |
| Powdered sugar | 3 cups |
| Rainbow sprinkles | For topping |

**1. Make cake:** Preheat oven to 325°F and generously coat Bundt pan with cooking spray.

**2.** In a large bowl, add cake mix, sour cream, milk, butter, vanilla, and eggs, and whisk to combine. Pour batter into the Bundt pan and smooth top with a spatula.

**3.** Bake cake until golden, 43 to 45 minutes. Let cool for 15 minutes in pan, then use a butter knife to run along the inside of the pan to release the cake from the pan. Then have a grown-up help you carefully invert the cake onto a cooling rack.

**4. Make frosting:** Add strawberries to a blender and puree until smooth. In a large bowl, whisk together pureed strawberries, cream cheese, and powdered sugar until smooth.

**5.** Pour frosting over cake and top with sprinkles.

# Nutella Pops

**Makes 6 • Total Time: 3 hours 15 minutes**

BEGINNER          PRO-IN-TRAINING          PRO

Turn your favorite chocolate-hazelnut spread into these adorable little pops. They taste like Fudgesicles...only better!

| Ingredients | Amount |
|---|---|
| **Whipped topping** | **1 cup** |
| **Milk** | **½ cup** |
| **Nutella** | **¼ cup** |

1. In a medium bowl, whisk together whipped topping, milk, and Nutella until combined. Pour mixture into six paper cups.

2. Top each cup with a small square of aluminum foil. Using a paring knife, cut a small slit in the middle of each.

3. Insert a Popsicle stick through each slit, and freeze mixture until firm, 3 hours.

4. When ready to serve, snip off a bit of the cup and peel off pop.

**What You'll Need**

Medium Bowl

Whisk

3-Ounce Paper Cups

Aluminum Foil

Paring Knife

Popsicle Sticks

Scissors

# Chapter 7

# FAN-TASTICS!

Get inspired by your favorite shows and characters!

# Captain's Cookie Cake

**Serves 12 • Total Time: 1 hour 40 minutes**

BEGINNER     PRO-IN-TRAINING     **PRO**

This giant red, white, and blue chocolate chip cookie is the perfect tribute to Captain America and his trusty shield. Disclaimer: This shield is not indestructible.

| Ingredients | Amount |
| --- | --- |
| **For the cookie** | |
| **Butter** | 1½ cups (3 sticks), softened |
| **Granulated sugar** | 1 cup |
| **Brown sugar** | 1 cup, packed |
| **Large eggs** | 2 |
| **Pure vanilla extract** | 2 teaspoons |
| **All-purpose flour** | 4 cups |
| **Baking powder** | 2 teaspoons |
| **Baking soda** | 1½ teaspoons |
| **Kosher salt** | 2 teaspoons |
| **Semisweet chocolate chips** | 4 cups |
| **For the buttercream** | |
| **Butter** | 2 cups (4 sticks), softened |
| **Powdered sugar** | 8 cups |
| **Pure vanilla extract** | 2 teaspoons |
| **Kosher salt** | ¼ teaspoon |
| **Heavy cream** | ½ cup |
| **Red and blue food coloring** | |

## What You'll Need

- Large Baking Sheet
- Parchment Paper
- 3 Large Bowls
- Oven Mitts
- Mixer
- Spatula
- 3 Medium Bowls
- 3 Piping Bags
- 2 Small Star Tips
- Medium Star Tip
- Star Cookie Cutter

1. **Make cookie:** Preheat oven to 350°F and line a large baking sheet with parchment paper. In a large bowl using a hand mixer or in the bowl of a stand mixer, beat together butter and sugars until light and fluffy. Add eggs and vanilla and beat until combined.

2. In another large bowl, stir together flour, baking powder, baking soda, and salt. Add dry ingredients to wet ingredients and beat just until combined. Fold in chocolate chips.

3. Place dough on baking sheet and form into a large circle, about 12 inches wide. Bake until almost set in the middle, 30 minutes (it will continue to set as it cools, so don't overbake it!). Let cool completely.

4. **Meanwhile, make buttercream:** In a large bowl using a hand mixer or in the bowl of a stand mixer, beat butter until smooth. Scrape down the sides with a spatula, add powdered sugar, and beat until smooth. Add vanilla, salt, and heavy cream and beat until well combined.

5. Divide frosting into three medium bowls (you'll need about half for the red; a quarter each for blue and white). Dye one bowl red, one bowl blue, and keep the third white.

6. **Pipe buttercream:** Transfer white frosting to a piping bag fitted with a small open star tip. Using a star cookie cutter as a guide, pipe dots to form a star in the middle of the cookie cake.

7. Transfer blue frosting to a piping bag fitted with a small open star tip. Pipe dots to form a circle around the star, filling in the triangles of the star as well.

8. Transfer red frosting to a piping bag fitted with a medium open star tip. Pipe small dots to form 2 red frosting circles around the blue, then pipe 2 circles of white around the red. Finish with 3 circles of red around the white.

If you want the giant frosted cookie but don't want to deal with piping a bunch of stars, pipe a peace sign, spell your name, or just spread a bunch of frosting on top and go nuts with sprinkles!

If you'd like larger servings, pipe the mixture into glasses, top with a sprinkling of crushed Oreos, and serve with a spoon.

# Grey Stuff

**Makes 55 • Total Time: 15 minutes**

BEGINNER　　PRO-IN-TRAINING　　PRO

The "grey stuff" Lumière sings about in *Beauty and the Beast* was probably meant to be a pâté, but we prefer our unofficial version of the sweet treat served at Disney theme parks.

**What You'll Need**

Large Bowl

Whisk

Spatula

Piping Bag

Large Star Tip

| Ingredients | Amount |
|---|---|
| **For the "grey stuff"** | |
| **Instant vanilla pudding** | 1 (3.4–ounce) package |
| **Instant chocolate pudding** | 2 tablespoons |
| **Whole milk** | 1⅓ cups, cold |
| **Whipped topping** | 1 (8–ounce) container |
| **Oreos** | 10, finely crushed (about 1 cup) |
| **For serving** | |
| **Oreos** | 55, whole |
| **White pearl sprinkles** | For decorating |

**1.** In a large bowl, combine vanilla and chocolate pudding. Add milk and whisk until it starts to thicken and no clumps remain. Refrigerate until set, 5 minutes.

**2.** Once pudding is set, use a spatula to fold in whipped topping and crushed Oreos. Transfer mixture to a piping bag fitted with a large open star tip.

**3.** Pipe grey stuff onto whole Oreos and decorate with pearl sprinkles.

# Princess Cupcakes

Makes 12 • Total Time: 40 minutes

BEGINNER     PRO-IN-TRAINING     PRO

No one could forget Cinderella's iconic blue ball gown. Now you can recreate it in cake form—glass slipper not included.

| Ingredients | Amount |
| --- | --- |
| Vanilla cake mix | 1 box, plus ingredients called for on box |
| Vanilla frosting | 3 (16-ounce) tubs |
| Blue food coloring | 8 to 10 drops |
| Large marshmallows | 12 |
| Mini marshmallows | 24 |
| Blue gel icing | 2 tubes |

**What You'll Need**

Muffin Tin

Cupcake Liners

Ice-Cream Scoop

Oven Mitts

Large Microwave-Safe Measuring Cup

Spatula

Baking Sheet

Parchment Paper

Wire Rack

1. Line a 12-cup muffin tin with cupcake liners. Prepare cupcakes according to package instructions. Let cool completely.

**2.** Spoon frosting into a large, microwave-safe liquid measuring cup. Add blue food coloring, stirring until combined. Continue adding food coloring until desired blue is reached.

**3.** Line a baking sheet with parchment paper and top with a wire rack. Place cupcakes upside down onto the rack, about an inch apart. Take a marshmallow, swipe one end with a little frosting, and gently place on the center of each upside-down cupcake, forming the base of Cinderella's gown.

**4.** Place the remaining frosting in the microwave, heating it for 20 to 25 seconds, then stir. It should be easily pourable.

**5.** Pour frosting on top of each cupcake, pouring directly over the marshmallow and slowly spiraling outward, until the cupcake is coated entirely. If the cupcake shows through the frosting, give it a second coating.

**6.** Before the frosting sets, place 2 mini marshmallows on the sides of each top marshmallow to create the puffy sleeves. Set aside for 10 minutes, so the frosting can set completely. Use gel icing to draw Cinderella's neckline and waistline. Beneath that, finish by drawing two rows of ruffles on the cupcake itself.

# Cookie Lover's Popcorn

**Serves 6 · Total Time: 30 minutes**

BEGINNER          PRO-IN-TRAINING          PRO

Do you constantly crave sweets? Yeah, we feel that.

## What You'll Need

Large Bowl

Small Microwave-Safe Bowl

Spoon

Baking Sheet

| Ingredients | Amount |
| --- | --- |
| Microwave popcorn | 1 bag |
| White chocolate chips | 2 cups |
| Vegetable oil | 1 teaspoon |
| Blue food coloring | 8 to 10 drops |
| Mini chocolate chip cookies | 1½ cups, plus crushed cookies for topping |
| Mini Oreos | 1½ cups, plus crushed cookies for topping |
| Candy eyeballs | For topping |

1. Pop the popcorn according to package directions. Place popcorn in a large bowl, being careful to remove any unpopped kernels.

2. Combine white chocolate chips and vegetable oil in a small microwave-safe bowl and heat in 20-second intervals, stirring in between, until fully melted. Stir in blue food coloring.

3. Add about half the blue chocolate mixture to popcorn. Stir, adding more chocolate, until popcorn is evenly coated.

4. Stir in chocolate chip cookies and Oreos. Spread onto a baking sheet in an even layer and top with candy eyeballs and crushed cookies.

5. Refrigerate 20 to 25 minutes before serving.

# Kevin & Bob Oreos

**Makes 12 • Total Time: 40 minutes**

BEGINNER        PRO-IN-TRAINING        PRO

It's hard not to crack a smile while decorating these little guys. The goofier, the better—just like the actual Minions.

| Ingredients | Amount |
| --- | --- |
| White chocolate chips | 2 cups |
| Coconut oil | 1 tablespoon |
| Yellow food coloring | 4 or 5 drops |
| Oreos | 12 |
| Black cookie icing | 1 tube |
| Candy eyeballs | 24 |

**1.** Line a baking sheet with parchment paper. In a medium bowl, combine white chocolate chips, coconut oil, and yellow food coloring. Microwave on 50 percent power in 30-second intervals until the chocolate has melted. Stir until smooth.

**2.** Using a fork, toss each Oreo in the yellow chocolate mixture until fully coated, and transfer to the baking sheet. Let chocolate harden, 10 minutes.

**3.** Use cookie icing to pipe glasses and mouth, then press candy eyes on top of glasses.

### What You'll Need

Baking Sheet

Parchment Paper

Medium Bowl

Spatula

Fork

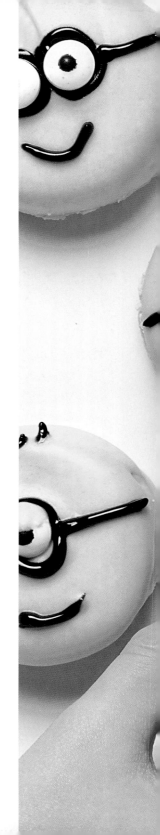

# Happiest Pretzels on Earth

**Makes 4 · Total Time: 35 minutes**

BEGINNER        PRO-IN-TRAINING        PRO

These adorable big-eared Mickey Mouse—inspired snacks taste just like your favorite concession-stand soft pretzel. Bonus: They make your kitchen smell amazing.

| Ingredients | Amount |
| --- | --- |
| Crescent roll dough | 2 (8-ounce) tubes |
| Baking soda | ⅓ cup |
| Warm water | 3 cups |
| Water | 1 tablespoon |
| Coarse salt | For sprinkling |
| Yellow mustard | For serving |

**What You'll Need**

Baking Sheet

Parchment Paper

Pizza Wheel

Shallow Bowl

Whisk

Pastry Brush

Oven Mitts

**1.** Preheat oven to 375°F and line a baking sheet with parchment paper. Roll out crescent dough and pinch seams together. Orient the dough so that the wide side is facing you, and use a pizza wheel to slice into 8 equally long strips.

**2.** Gently roll a strip of dough so that instead of a strip, it comes to form a long, thin tube.

**3.** Shape tube into a large circle on the prepared baking sheet. Roll a second strip into a long, thin tube, then slice in half and form the halves into small circles for ears. Place them onto the prepared baking sheet so they are touching the big circle and will bake as one.

**4.** In a shallow bowl, combine baking soda and warm water and whisk until dissolved. Brush all over crescent pretzel. Sprinkle with coarse salt.

**5.** Bake until pretzels are puffed and golden, and serve with mustard.

# Arendelle Fudge

**Serves 16 • Total Time: 3 hours 15 minutes**

BEGINNER · PRO-IN-TRAINING · PRO

Inspired by Elsa's vibrant blue dress, this fudge is eye-catching, to say the least. Although these sweet squares don't have any actual magical powers, they always manage to brighten the mood. (Maybe it's all the sprinkles.)

| Ingredients | Amount |
| --- | --- |
| Cooking spray | For pan |
| White chocolate chips | 3½ cups |
| Sweetened condensed milk | 1 (14-ounce) can |
| Pure vanilla extract | ½ teaspoon |
| Blue food coloring | 8 to 10 drops |
| Sprinkles | For topping |

1. Line an 8x8-inch pan with parchment paper and grease with cooking spray. In a large microwave-safe bowl, combine white chocolate and sweetened condensed milk. Microwave on medium power 1-minute intervals, stirring with a fork after each minute.

2. Add vanilla and blue food coloring to bowl and stir until fully incorporated. Pour into baking pan and top with sprinkles.

3. Refrigerate until fudge is set, 3 hours. Cut into squares and serve.

**Warning!**
The bowl will be hot! Use oven mitts after microwaving to handle bowl.

**What You'll Need**

Baking Pan

Parchment Paper

Large Microwave-Safe Bowl

Fork

Oven Mitts

# Exploding Bonbons

**Makes 20 • Total Time: 1 hour 35 minutes**

BEGINNER     PRO-IN-TRAINING     PRO

Okay, we might not be able to conjure up any spells like Harry, but we have the next best thing: Pop Rocks. These magical bonbons crackle as soon as you bite into them.

| Ingredients | Amount |
| --- | --- |
| Cooking spray | For pan |
| Vanilla cake mix | 1 box, plus ingredients called for on box |
| Vanilla icing | ¾ cup |
| Red, blue, purple, and green Pop Rocks | 1 package of each |
| White chocolate chips | 2 cups |
| Refined coconut oil | 2 teaspoons |
| Yellow food coloring | 3 drops |

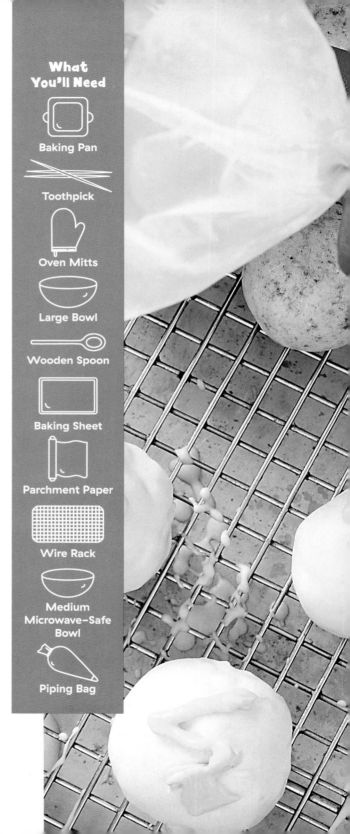

**What You'll Need**

Baking Pan

Toothpick

Oven Mitts

Large Bowl

Wooden Spoon

Baking Sheet

Parchment Paper

Wire Rack

Medium Microwave-Safe Bowl

Piping Bag

1. Preheat oven to 350°F and grease a 9x13-inch pan with cooking spray.

2. Prepare cake mix according to package directions, transfer batter to baking pan, and bake until a toothpick inserted in the center comes out clean, 25 minutes. Let cool completely.

3. Crumble cake into a large bowl, making sure to break apart any large pieces. Add icing and stir until fully incorporated. Line a baking sheet with parchment paper, then place a wire cooling rack on baking sheet.

4. Roll cake mixture into 20 small balls about the size of ping-pong balls. Make a well in each with your thumb and transfer balls to the wire rack. Pour Pop Rocks into wells and seal with more cake mixture, rolling one more time to make sure they are round and sealed.

5. Place baking sheet in freezer for 30 minutes, until bonbons are firm.

6. Combine white chocolate chips and coconut oil in a medium microwave-safe bowl. Microwave in 30-second increments, stirring in between. Spoon melted white chocolate over chilled bonbons until all are coated.

7. Mix yellow food coloring into remaining white chocolate and transfer to piping bag or resealable plastic bag, then cut off the very tip to create a small hole.

8. Decorate each cake ball with a lightning bolt, then transfer to the freezer for 10 minutes.

Chapter 8

parties!

It's time to
celebrate!

## What You'll Need

Baking Pan

Parchment Paper

Large Heatproof Bowl

Saucepan

Whisk

Spatula

Toothpick

Oven Mitts

Chef's Knife

Rimmed Baking Sheet

Medium Heatproof Bowl

# Ghost Brownies

**Makes 16 · Total Time: 2 hours**

BEGINNER          PRO-IN-TRAINING          PRO

Make these brownies your own by adding your favorite Halloween candy to the mix.

| Ingredients | Amount |
| --- | --- |
| Butter | ½ cup (1 stick), cut into cubes, plus more for pan |
| Semisweet chocolate chips | 1¼ cups |
| Granulated sugar | ¾ cup |
| Brown sugar | ¾ cup, packed |
| Large eggs | 3 |
| Unsweetened cocoa powder | ¼ cup |
| Kosher salt | ½ teaspoon |
| All-purpose flour | 1 cup |
| Reese's Peanut Butter Cups | 5, chopped |
| M&M's | ½ cup |
| Candy corn | ½ cup |
| Large marshmallows | 16 |
| White chocolate chips | 1½ cups |
| Coconut oil | 3 tablespoons |
| Black decorating gel | For decorating |

According to a 2019 study, the most popular Halloween candy in America is Skittles. Americans purchase 3.3 million pounds of the rainbow candies every Halloween.

**1. Make brownies:** Preheat oven to 350°F. Brush a 9x9–inch baking pan with butter and line with parchment paper, leaving an overhang on two sides. Butter the parchment paper.

**2.** In a large heatproof bowl set over a saucepan of simmering water, melt ½ cup butter and chocolate chips, stirring until smooth. Remove bowl from heat and whisk in sugars. Whisk in eggs, one at a time, until fully combined.

**3.** Whisk in cocoa powder and salt, then fold in flour, chopped Reese's, M&M's, and candy corn. Pour batter into baking pan.

**4.** Bake until a toothpick inserted in center comes out with moist crumbs, 35 minutes. Let cool completely.

**5. Make ghosts:** Use the overhanging parchment paper to lift brownies out of pan, then cut into 16 squares. Arrange squares on a parchment–paper–lined rimmed baking sheet. Top each square with a marshmallow.

**6.** In a medium heatproof bowl, microwave white chocolate chips with coconut oil until melted. Stir until smooth.

**7.** Drizzle chocolate over each marshmallow–topped brownie. Refrigerate until set, about 10 minutes.

**8.** Use black decorating gel to create eyes and a mouth on each marshmallow.

# Giant Reese's Stuffed Skillet Cookie

**Serves 10 • Total Time: 35 minutes**

BEGINNER     PRO-IN-TRAINING     PRO

When you have an excess of peanut butter cups from trick-or-treating, the most logical thing to do is to stuff them into a giant skillet cookie and top it with ice cream.

**What You'll Need**

- Cast-Iron Skillet
- Large Bowl
- Mixer
- Oven Mitts
- Small Microwave-Safe Bowl

| Ingredients | Amount |
| --- | --- |
| Cooking spray | For pan |
| Creamy peanut butter | ¾ cup, divided |
| Butter | ½ cup (1 stick) |
| Brown sugar | ½ cup, packed |
| Granulated sugar | ¼ cup |
| Large egg | 1 |
| Pure vanilla extract | 1 teaspoon |
| All-purpose flour | 1½ cups |
| Baking soda | ½ teaspoon |
| Kosher salt | ½ teaspoon |
| Reese's Cups | 13 |
| Mini Reese's Cups | 1½ cups, plus more for topping |
| Reese's Pieces | ¼ cup, plus more for topping |
| Melted chocolate | For topping |
| Ice cream | For topping |

1. Preheat oven to 350°F and grease a 10-inch cast-iron skillet with cooking spray. In a large bowl using a hand mixer or in the bowl of a stand mixer, combine ½ cup peanut butter, butter, and sugars and beat on medium until mixture is light and fluffy. Add egg and vanilla and mix until thoroughly combined, then add flour, baking soda, and salt and mix until just combined.

2. Press half the cookie dough onto the bottom and up the sides of the skillet. Press Reese's Cups into dough, then top with remaining cookie dough. Gently press in 1½ cups mini Reese's Cups and ¼ cup Reese's Pieces.

3. Bake until cookie is set, 15 to 20 minutes.

4. In a small microwave-safe bowl, microwave remaining ¼ cup peanut butter until melty, 20 seconds.

5. Drizzle cookie with melted peanut butter and melted chocolate, and top with more candy. Serve with ice cream.

# Sugar Cookie Truffles

**Makes 15 • Total Time: 45 minutes**

BEGINNER          PRO-IN-TRAINING          PRO

Transform your extra holiday cookies (there are always so many!) into candy-like treats.

| Ingredients | Amount |
| --- | --- |
| Baked sugar cookies | 15 |
| Cream cheese | 1 (8-ounce) block, softened |
| Pure vanilla extract | 1 teaspoon |
| Kosher salt | Pinch |
| Coconut oil | 2 teaspoons |
| White chocolate chips | 1¼ cups |
| Christmas sprinkles | For topping |

**1.** Line a small baking sheet with parchment paper. In a large food processor, pulse cookies until sandy. Or place cookies in a large resealable plastic bag and use a rolling pin to crush cookies into crumbs.

**2.** In a large bowl, stir to combine crushed cookies, cream cheese, vanilla, and salt. Using a small cookie scoop, form cookie mixture into small balls and place on baking sheet. Repeat until all mixture is used, then place baking sheet in freezer for 10 minutes.

**3.** Meanwhile, in a medium microwave-safe bowl, combine coconut oil and white chocolate chips. Microwave on low in 30-second intervals, stirring with a fork in between, until white chocolate is completely melted.

**4.** When the balls are chilled, dip them in white chocolate and return to baking sheet. Decorate immediately with Christmas sprinkles. When all truffles are dipped and decorated, return to freezer for 10 minutes to set.

## What You'll Need

Small Baking Sheet

Parchment Paper

Resealable Plastic Bag

Rolling Pin

Large Bowl

Small Cookie Scoop

Medium Microwave-Safe Bowl

Fork

# Santa Hat Pancakes

**Serves 4 to 6 • Total Time: 30 minutes**

BEGINNER ——●—— PRO-IN-TRAINING —— PRO

We've got Christmas breakfast on lock, thanks to these festive pancakes.

| Ingredients | Amount |
|---|---|
| Pancake mix | Plus ingredients called for on box |
| Pure vanilla extract | 1 teaspoon |
| Butter | For pan |
| Strawberries | 6, stem side cut |
| Whipped topping | |
| Powdered sugar | For topping |
| Maple syrup | For serving |

**1.** In a large bowl, prepare pancake mix according to package directions, then stir in vanilla. For easy pouring, transfer batter to a clean squeeze bottle.

**2.** In a large nonstick skillet over medium heat, melt butter. Squeeze small rounds of batter into pan and cook until bubbles form in batter and begin to pop, about 1 minute. Flip and cook until golden on the other side, about 1 minute more. Transfer to a plate and cover with foil to keep warm.

**3.** On a serving platter, stack three mini pancakes. Spread whipped topping on top, then place a strawberry on top. Add a tiny dollop of whipped topping to the tip of the strawberry.

**4.** Sprinkle with powdered sugar and serve with maple syrup.

Follow directions for preparing about 16 pancakes.

**What You'll Need**

Large Bowl

Squeeze Bottle

Large Nonstick Skillet

Turner

Plate

Aluminum Foil

Butter Knife

Using a squeeze bottle is the easiest way to control the size of your pancakes. But if you don't have one, you could use a small cookie scoop instead.

# Pigs in a Blanket Wreath

Serves 12 • Total Time: 35 minutes

BEGINNER     PRO-IN-TRAINING     PRO

It's not a party without pigs in a blanket. In this holiday version, rosemary sprigs really brings the "wreath" to life.

| Ingredients | Amount |
| --- | --- |
| Refrigerated crescent rolls | 1 (8-ounce) tube |
| Mini hot dogs | 24 |
| Dijon mustard | ¼ cup |
| Large egg | 1 |
| Water | 1 tablespoon |
| Poppy seeds | 2 teaspoons |
| Rosemary sprigs | For decorating |
| Ketchup | For serving |

**What You'll Need**

Large Baking Sheet

Parchment Paper

Knife

2 Small Bowls

Whisk

Basting Brush

Oven Mitts

1. Preheat oven to 375°F and line a large baking sheet with parchment paper.

2. Slice each crescent roll lengthwise into thirds to make 3 long, super-skinny triangles. With a basting brush, coat each piece all over with Dijon mustard. Place a mini hot dog on the thick end of each triangle and roll it up.

3. **Make egg wash:** In a small bowl, whisk together egg and water until frothy.

4. Arrange the pigs in a blanket, side by side, in a circle on the baking sheet. They should be touching! Use the basting brush to brush egg wash over crescent dough, then sprinkle with poppy seeds.

5. Bake 15 to 20 minutes, until crescents are golden. Let cool for at least 20 minutes.

6. Arrange rosemary sprigs around the inside of the wreath and place a small bowl filled with ketchup in the center.

## Cooking With Grandma

**Learn how to make tamales with Aminta!**

Starting at a very young age, Aminta Santamaria was curious in the kitchen. She taught herself how to cook by observing others and not giving up. Today she runs her own restaurant in El Salvador called Panes Migueleños Santamaria.

**"Cooking is the most beautiful thing,"** Aminta says. The lessons she wants to pass on to her grandchildren are: **(1)** You can learn to cook just by watching. **(2)** Give food "that touch of love." **(3)** Be consistent. **(4)** Keep trying and don't give up.

# Tamales de Elote

**Makes 40 • Total Time: 1 hour 45 minutes**

BEGINNER      PRO-IN-TRAINING      PRO

Many Latin American countries have their own spin on the tamale. This is a traditional Salvadoran recipe. "Elote" means "corn on the cob" and this dish is pronounced *tuh–MA–lays de eh–LO–tay*.

| Ingredients | Amount |
| --- | --- |
| Corn | 10 ears (plus their husks) |
| Kosher salt | |
| Butter | 4 tablespoons, melted |
| Granulated sugar | 1 to 2 tablespoons |
| Maseca (instant masa corn flour) | 1 cup |
| Crema | For serving |

**1.** Shuck corn, saving husks for later. With a grown–up's help, use a knife to remove kernels from cobs. Save cobs for later.

**2.** Working in batches, blend corn kernels with a pinch of salt until very finely ground, then transfer to a large bowl.

**3.** Stir in butter, then season with sugar. Add ½ cup maseca and mix until combined, then gradually add up to ½ cup more maseca, until mixture is still moist and soft but able to hold its shape.

**4.** Spread about 2 tablespoons of the mixture inside a corn husk, then fold ends to completely wrap around the dough. Repeat with remaining corn mixture.

**5.** To a large pot, add corncobs, then fill the bottom of the pot with water so the water reaches about halfway up the cobs. Stand tamales up on top of cobs, then cover with any leftover corn husks. (This helps trap the steam!)

**6.** Boil until corn filling is firm and easily separates from the husks, 30 to 50 minutes.

**7.** Serve with crema.

You can also use sour cream and thin it out with a little heavy cream.

**What You'll Need**

Knife

Blender

Large Bowl

Spoon

Large Pot

# Buddy the Elf Cookies

**Makes 10 • Total Time: 20 minutes**

BEGINNER          PRO-IN-TRAINING          PRO

Have you ever been tempted to try spaghetti with chocolate syrup, maple syrup, marshmallows, M&M's, and sprinkles (aka Buddy's breakfast in the movie *Elf*)? Don't do it! Make these crunchy cookies—which resemble candy-loaded piles of pasta—instead.

## What You'll Need

Microwave-Safe Bowl

Spatula

Large Bowl

Parchment Paper

Baking Sheet

Spoon

| Ingredients | Amount |
| --- | --- |
| White chocolate chips | 1 (12-ounce) bag |
| Crunchy chow mein noodles | 3 cups |
| Marshmallow bits | ½ cup |
| Chocolate syrup | For drizzling |
| Rainbow sprinkles | For topping |

**1.** In a microwave-safe bowl, microwave white chocolate in 30-second intervals, stirring in between, until melted, 2 minutes. Pour into a large bowl and use a spatula to toss with chow mein noodles and marshmallow bits.

**2.** Drop spoonfuls of mixture onto a parchment-lined baking sheet. Drizzle with fudge sauce and top with rainbow sprinkles. Refrigerate until set, 15 minutes.

# Holiday Cookie Pops

**Makes 15 • Total Time: 30 minutes**

BEGINNER      PRO-IN-TRAINING      PRO

Everyone decorates Christmas sugar cookies with icing. Not enough people roll them in sugar and turn them into pops. Pro tip: Dunk 'em in your hot cocoa.

| Ingredients | Amount |
| --- | --- |
| Refrigerated sugar cookie dough | 1 (16.5–ounce) tube |
| Christmas sprinkles | For decorating |

**1.** Preheat oven to 350°F and line two large baking sheets with parchment paper.

**2.** Scoop 1 tablespoon of dough and roll into a small ball. Repeat until all the cookie dough is used.

**3.** Roll cookie dough balls in sprinkles, then insert Popsicle sticks into the centers. Transfer to prepared baking sheets, spacing cookies at least 2 inches apart.

**4.** Bake according to package instructions, usually 12 to 15 minutes.  The cookies will flatten as they bake.

**5.** Let cool completely before serving. (A warm cookie will break off the Popsicle stick!)

Alexis Morillo

Lena Abraham

# Thank You!

To the incredible Delish team, which has so much wisdom to offer. Thank you from the bottom of my heart to all the wonderful humans who brought this book to life: Senior Food Editor Lena Abraham, Food Director Lauren Miyashiro, Food Editor Makinze Gore, and Contributing Test Kitchen Assistant Justin Sullivan; Deputy Editor Sarah Weinberg, Senior Features Editor Tess Koman, News Editor Kristin Salaky, and Contributing News Writer Alexis Morillo; Art Director Allie Folino, Designer Sabrina Contratti, Director of Content Operations Lindsey Ramsey, and cover team Works Well With Others and Lindsay Funston. To our mentors at Hearst, including Kate Lewis, Jacqueline Deval, Nicole Fisher, and Brian Madden.

To my father, whose guidance I miss every single day; to my mother, who is still steering me right; to my husband, Scott, and my children, Spencer, Teddy, and Everett, who are always teaching me how to do better and love more.

Lauren Miyashiro

Allie Folino

Lindsey Ramsey

Makinze Gore

Tess Koman

# Credits

**Front Cover Photography**
Chelsea Kyle

**Front Cover Typography**
Erik Bernstein

**Cover Food Styling**
Micah Morton

**Cover Art Direction**
Works Well With Others
Design Group

**Joanna Saltz Headshots**
Allie Holloway

**Illustrations**
Allie Folino

**Copy Editors**
Elzy Kolb
Briehn Trumbauer

**Interior Photography**
Yossy Arefi: 172

Erik Bernstein: 2–3, 10–11, 28–29, 52–53, 58–59, 62–63, 72–73, 90–91, 104–105, 120–121, 128–129, 144–145, 150–151, 168–169, 192

Andrew Bui: 33, 40–41, 44–45, 71, 76–77, 82, 87, 98–99, 102–103, 108–109, 116–117, 126–127, 140–141, 158–159, 178, 180–181

Ethan Calabrese: 12–13, 101, 113, 136–137

Suzanne Clements: 60–61

Parker Feierbach: 16, 18–19, 30–31, 46–47, 78–81, 84–85, 94–95, 106–107, 118

Emily Hlavac Green: 14–15, 64–65, 74–75, 124–125, 133, 134–135, 156–157, 162–163

Allie Holloway: 4

Chelsea Kyle: 110

David A. Land: 26–27, 67, 88–89, 130–131, 146, 166–167

Lucy Schaeffer: 22–23, 24–25, 34–35, 36, 38–39, 42–43, 48, 50–51, 54–55, 56–57, 92–93, 114–115, 123, 138, 142–143, 148–149, 152–153, 154, 160–161, 165, 170–171, 174, 177, 182–183, 184

Delish Team: 186

Grandma Knows Best: Courtesy of Laura Vegas, Aminta Santamaria

Minions: Universal Studios Licensing LLC

# Index

Copyright © 2021 by Hearst Magazine Media, Inc.

Cover design by Works Well With Others Design Group
Book design by Sabrina Contratti

Library of Congress Cataloging–in–Publication Data available on request

10 9 8 7 6 5 4 3 2 1

Published by Hearst Home, an imprint of Hearst Books/Hearst Magazine Media, Inc.
300 W 57th Street
New York, NY 10019

Delish, Hearst Home, the Hearst Home logo, and Hearst Books are registered trademarks of Hearst Communications, Inc.

For information about custom editions, special sales, premium and corporate purchases: hearst.com/magazines/hearst–books

Printed in Canada
ISBN 978-1-950785-43-8

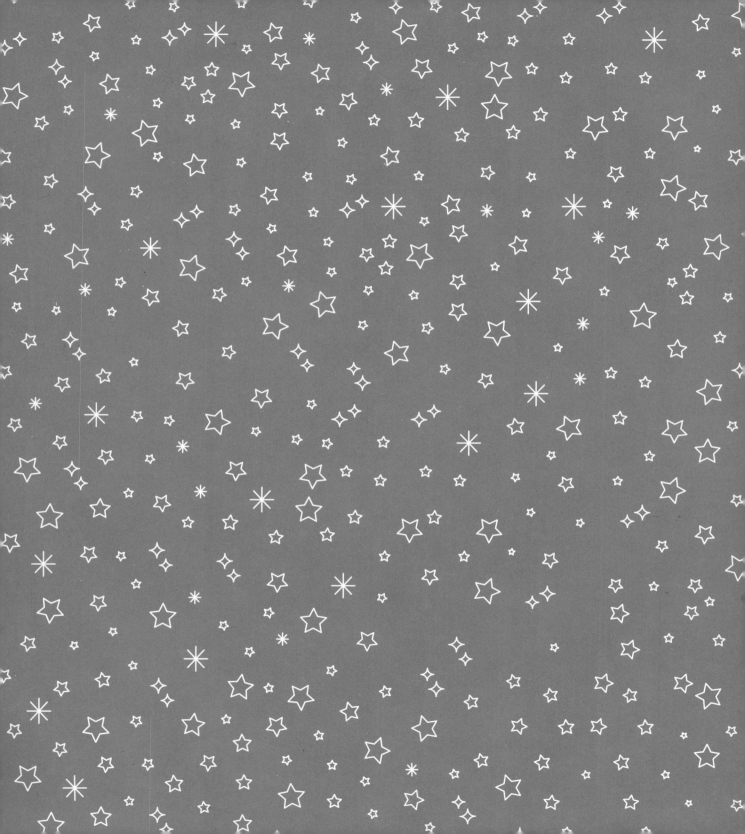